Gretchen Bitterlin
Dennis Johnson
Donna Price
Sylvia Ramirez
K. Lynn Savage, Series Editor

Ventures 3

STUDENT'S BOOK

CAMBRIDGE
UNIVERSITY PRESS

CAMBRIDGE UNIVERSITY PRESS
Cambridge, New York, Melbourne, Madrid, Cape Town, Singapore, São Paulo, Delhi

Cambridge University Press
32 Avenue of the Americas, New York, NY 10013-2473, USA

www.cambridge.org
Information on this title: www.cambridge.org/9780521600996

First published 2008

Printed in the United States of America

A catalog record for this publication is available from the British Library

ISBN 978-0-521-60099-6 pack consisting of Student's Book and Audio CD
ISBN 978-0-521-67960-2 Workbook
ISBN 978-0-521-69891-7 pack consisting of Teacher's Edition and Teacher's Toolkit Audio CD/CD-ROM
ISBN 978-0-521-67730-1 CDs (Audio)
ISBN 978-0-521-67731-8 Cassettes
ISBN 978-0-521-67585-7 Add Ventures

Art direction, book design, photo research, and layout services: Adventure House, NYC
Audio production: Richard LePage and Associates

Authors' acknowledgments

The authors would like to acknowledge and thank focus group participants and reviewers for their insightful comments, as well as CUP editorial, marketing, and production staffs, whose thorough research and attention to detail have resulted in a quality product.

The publishers would also like to extend their particular thanks to the following reviewers and consultants for their valuable insights and suggestions:

Francesca Armendaris, North Orange County Community College District, Anaheim, California; **Alex A. Baez**, The Texas Professional Development Group, Austin, Texas; **Kit Bell**, LAUSD Division of Adult and Career Education, Los Angeles, California; **Rose Anne Cleary**, Catholic Migration Office, Diocese of Brooklyn, Brooklyn, New York; **Inga Cristi**, Pima Community College Adult Education, Tucson, Arizona; **Kay De Gennaro**, West Valley Occupational Center, Woodland Hills, California; **Patricia DeJesus-Lopez**, Illinois Community College Board, Springfield, Illinois; **Magali Apareaida Morais Duignan**, Augusta State University, Augusta, Georgia; **Gayle Fagan**, Harris County Department of Education, Houston, Texas; **Lisa A. Fears**, Inglewood Community Adult School, Inglewood, California; **Jas Gill**, English Language Institute at the University of British Columbia, Vancouver, British Columbia, Canada; **Elisabeth Goodwin**, Pima Community College Adult Education, Tucson, Arizona; **Carolyn Grimaldi**, Center for Immigrant Education and Training, LaGuardia Community College, Long Island City, New York; **Masha Gromyko**, Pima Community College Adult Education, Tucson, Arizona; **Jennifer M. Herrin**, Albuquerque TVI Community College, Albuquerque, New Mexico; **Giang T. Hoang**, Evans Community Adult School, Los Angeles, California; **Karen Hribar**, LAUSD West Valley Occupational Center, Los Angeles, California; **Patricia Ishill**, Union County College, Union County, New Jersey; **Dr. Stephen G. Karel**, McKinley Community School for Adults, Honolulu, Hawaii; **Aaron Kelly**, North Orange County Community College District, Anaheim, California; **Dan Kiernan**, Metro Skills Center, LAUSD, Los Angeles, California; **Kirsten Kilcup**, Green River Community College, Auburn, Washington; **Tom Knutson**, New York Association for New Americans, Inc., New York, New York; **Liz Koenig-Golombek**, LAUSD, Los Angeles, California; **Anita Lemonis**, West Valley Occupational Center, Los Angeles, California; **Lia Lerner**, Burbank Adult School, Burbank, California; **Susan Lundquist**, Pima Community College Adult Education, Tucson, Arizona; **Dr. Amal Mahmoud**, Highline Community College, Des Moines, Washington; **Fatiha Makloufi**, Hostos Community College, Bronx, New York; **Judith Martin-Hall**, Indian River Community College, Fort Pierce, Florida; **Gwen Mayer**, Van Nuys Community Adult School, Los Angeles, California; **Lois Miller**, Pima Community College Adult Education, Tucson, Arizona; **Vicki Moore**, El Monte-Rosemead Adult School, El Monte, California; **Jeanne Petrus-Rivera**, Cuyahoga Community College, Cleveland, Ohio; **Pearl W. Pigott**, Houston Community College, Houston, Texas; **Catherine Porter**, Adult Learning Resource Center, Des Plaines, Illinois; **Planaria Price**, Evans Community Adult School, Los Angeles, California; **James P. Regan**, NYC Board of Education, New York, New York; **Catherine M. Rifkin**, Florida Community College at Jacksonville, Jacksonville, Florida; **Amy Schneider**, Pacoima Skills Center, Los Angeles, California; **Bonnie Sherman**, Green River Community College, Auburn, Washington; **Julie Singer**, Garfield Community Adult School, Los Angeles, California; **Yilin Sun**, Seattle Central Community College, Seattle, Washington; **André Sutton**, Belmont Community Adult School, Los Angeles, California; **Deborah Thompson**, El Camino Real Community Adult School, Los Angeles, California; **Evelyn Trottier**, Basic Studies Division, Seattle Central Community College, Seattle, Washington; **Debra Un**, New York University, American Language Institute, New York, New York; **Jodie Morgan Vargas**, Orange County Public Schools, Orlando, Florida; **Christopher Wahl**, Hudson County Community College, Jersey City, New Jersey; **Ethel S. Watson**, Evans Community Adult School, Los Angeles, California; **Barbara Williams**; **Mimi Yang**, Belmont Community Adult School, Los Angeles, California; **Adèle Youmans**, Pima Community College Adult Education, Tucson, Arizona.

Scope and sequence

UNIT TITLE TOPIC	FUNCTIONS	LISTENING AND SPEAKING	VOCABULARY	GRAMMAR FOCUS
Welcome Unit pages 2–5	• Exchanging personal information • Introducing a classmate • Discussing goals	• Asking about personal information • Introducing a classmate • Asking about goals	• Review of time words	• Verb tense review – past, present continuous, simple present, and future
Unit 1 Personal information pages 6–17 Topic: Personality traits	• Describing and comparing likes and interests • Describing and discussing personality types	• Asking about and comparing preferences • Describing personality types	• Personal interests • Personality types	• Verbs + gerunds • Comparisons with *more than*, *less than*, *as much as*
Unit 2 At school pages 18–29 Topic: Study skills	• Discussing study problems and learning strategies • Offering advice • Inquiring about people's experiences	• Asking about study habits and learning strategies • Asking about someone's recent past	• Study problems • Learning strategies	• Present perfect with *How long; for* and *since* • Present perfect questions with *ever*; short answers
Review: Units 1 and 2 pages 30–31		• Understanding a conversation		
Unit 3 Friends and family pages 32–43 Topic: Neighbors	• Offering help • Agreeing and disagreeing • Giving reasons • Making a complaint • Making a request	• Asking about and describing problems • Giving reasons • Discussing borrowing and lending	• *borrow* vs. *lend* • Two-word verbs	• *because* and *because of* to give reasons • *enough* and *too*
Unit 4 Health pages 44–55 Topic: Healthful habits	• Discussing healthful foods and exercise • Describing events in the recent past • Describing past habits	• Asking about staying healthy • Asking about past and present health habits	• Healthful habits and routines • Medicinal plants	• Present perfect with *recently* and *lately* • *used to*
Review: Units 3 and 4 pages 56–57		• Understanding a conversation		
Unit 5 Around town pages 58–69 Topic: Community resources and events	• Discussing future plans • Describing actions based on expectations • Describing community events	• Asking about people's plans • Asking about people's expectations • Talking about community events	• Entertainment • Positive and negative adjectives	• Verbs + infinitives • Present perfect with *already* and *yet*

READING	WRITING	LIFE SKILLS	PRONUNCIATION
• Reading a paragraph about goals	• Writing sentences about your partner	• Talking about your goals	• Pronouncing key vocabulary
• Reading an article about personality and jobs • Predicting content from titles and pictures	• Writing a descriptive paragraph • Using adjectives	• Understanding a bar graph • Reading a personal ad	• Pronouncing key vocabulary
• Reading an article about strategies for learning English • Using context to identify parts of speech • Locating examples	• Writing an expository paragraph • Using examples to support your ideas	• Reading and understanding tips for taking tests • Talking about strategies for learning English	• Pronouncing key vocabulary
			• Stressing content words
• Reading a newsletter about a neighborhood watch • Identifying the main idea, facts, and examples	• Writing a letter of complaint • Supporting the main idea with examples	• Reading and understanding an ad for volunteers • Writing a letter of complaint	• Pronouncing key vocabulary
• Reading an article about healthful plants • Identifying the introduction and the conclusion • Identifying parts of word families	• Writing a descriptive paragraph • Completing a chart	• Completing a medical history form • Talking about how to stay healthy	• Pronouncing key vocabulary
			• Voiced and voiceless *th* sounds
• Reading a review of a concert • Using context to guess positive or negative connotations of words	• Writing an e-mail • Completing a graphic organizer	• Reading announcements about community events • Talking about community events	• Pronouncing key vocabulary

UNIT TITLE TOPIC	FUNCTIONS	LISTENING AND SPEAKING	VOCABULARY	GRAMMAR FOCUS
Unit 6 Time pages 70–81 Topic: Time management	• Prioritizing • Discussing how to manage time • Giving advice • Describing habits	• Prioritizing tasks • Asking about habits and daily activities • Contrasting good and weak time management	• Time-management words • Prefixes meaning *not* • Idioms with *time*	• Dependent clauses with *when* • Dependent clauses with *before* and *after*
Review: Units 5 and 6 pages 82–83		• Understanding a conversation		
Unit 7 Shopping pages 84–95 Topic: Saving and spending	• Making suggestions • Asking for and giving advice • Discussing financial concerns • Comparing banking services	• Asking and answering questions about buying on credit • Making suggestions and giving advice	• Banking and finances • *Noun + noun* combinations	• *could* and *should* • Gerunds after prepositions
Unit 8 Work pages 96–107 Topic: Finding a job	• Discussing work-related goals • Discussing ways to find a job • Identifying procedures involved with a job interview	• Talking about a job interview • Asking about ongoing activities	• Employment • Separable phrasal verbs	• Present perfect continuous • Separable phrasal verbs
Review: Units 7 and 8 pages 108–109		• Understanding a conversation		
Unit 9 Daily living pages 110–121 Topic: Community action	• Describing past activities • Describing past events	• Describing a crime • Describing past actions • Asking about an emergency • Discussing safety items	• Crimes • Emergency situations • Time phrases	• Past continuous • Past continuous and simple past with *when* and *while*
Unit 10 Leisure pages 122–133 Topic: Vacation plans	• Describing future possibility • Describing a sequence of events in the future	• Describing vacation plans • Asking about future possibility • Describing the sequence of future events	• Travel and vacation	• Future conditional clauses with *if* • Future clauses with *before* and *after*
Review: Units 9 and 10 pages 134–135		• Understanding a news report		

Projects **pages 136–140**
Self-assessments **pages 141–145**
Reference **pages 146–153**
   Grammar charts **pages 146–150**
   Irregular verbs **page 151**
   Grammar explanations **pages 152–153**
Self-study audio script **pages 154–161**

READING	WRITING	LIFE SKILLS	PRONUNCIATION
• Reading an article about being *on time* • Using dashes to introduce examples • Identifying words with prefixes meaning *not*	• Writing a descriptive paragraph about a good or a weak time manager • Using concluding phrases	• Reading and understanding a pie chart • Talking about how to manage time	• Pronouncing key vocabulary
			• Initial *st* sound
• Reading an article about credit card debt • Understanding a reading with problems and solutions	• Giving advice about saving money • Using *first*, *second*, *third*, and *finally* to organize ideas	• Reading and understanding a brochure comparing checking accounts • Talking about credit, credit cards, and debt	• Pronouncing key vocabulary
• Reading a blog about a job search • Scanning for specific information	• Writing a thank-you letter following a job interview • Understanding what to include in a thank-you letter	• Reading and understanding a chart comparing job growth • Preparing for a job interview	• Pronouncing key vocabulary
			• Linking sounds
• Reading an article about community action • Recognizing time phrases • Guessing meaning from context	• Writing about an emergency • Using *Who*, *What*, *When*, *Where*, *Why*, and *How*	• Reading and understanding a chart comparing safety in various U.S. states • Discussing emergency situations	• Pronouncing key vocabulary
• Reading an article about Alcatraz • Using clues to guess the meaning of words	• Writing about a tourist attraction • Using complex sentences to add variety	• Reading and understanding hotel brochures • Talking about travel arrangements	• Pronouncing key vocabulary
			• Unstressed vowel sound

To the teacher

What is *Ventures?*

Ventures is a five-level, standards-based, integrated-skills series for adult students. The five levels, which are Basic through Level Four, are for low-beginning literacy to high-intermediate students.

The *Ventures* series is flexible enough to be used in open enrollment, managed enrollment, and traditional programs. Its multilevel features support teachers who work with multilevel classes.

What components does *Ventures* have?

Student's Book with Self-study Audio CD

Each **Student's Book** contains a Welcome Unit and ten topic-focused units, plus five review units, one after every two units. Each unit has six skill-focused lessons. Projects, self-assessments, and a reference section are included at the back of the Student's Book.

- **Lessons** are self-contained, allowing for completion within a one-hour class period.
- **Review lessons** recycle, reinforce, and consolidate the materials presented in the previous two units and include a pronunciation activity.
- **Projects** offer community-building opportunities for students to work together – using the Internet or completing a task, such as making a poster or a book.
- **Self-assessments** are an important part of students' learning and success. They give students an opportunity to evaluate and reflect on their learning as well as a tool to support learner persistence.
- The **Self-study Audio CD** is included at the back of the Student's Book. The material on the CD is indicated in the Student's Book by an icon SELF-STUDY AUDIO CD .

Teacher's Edition with Teacher's Toolkit Audio CD/CD-ROM

The interleaved **Teacher's Edition** walks instructors step-by-step through the stages of a lesson.

- Included are learner-persistence and community-building tasks as well as teaching tips, expansion activities, and ways to expand a lesson to two or three instructional hours.

- The Student's Book answer key is included on the interleaved pages in the Teacher's Edition.
- The Teacher's Toolkit Audio CD/CD-ROM contains additional reproducible material for teacher support. Included are picture dictionary cards and worksheets (Levels 1 and 2), extended reading worksheets (Levels 3 and 4), tests with audio, and student self-assessments for portfolio assessment. Reproducible sheets also include cooperative learning activities. These activities reinforce the materials presented in the Student's Book and develop social skills, including those identified by SCANS[1] as being highly valued by employers.
- The unit, midterm, and final tests are found on both the Teacher's Toolkit Audio CD/CD-ROM and in the Teacher's Edition. The tests include listening, vocabulary, grammar, reading, and writing sections.

Audio Program

The *Ventures* series includes a **Class Audio** and a **Student Self-study Audio** SELF-STUDY AUDIO CD . The Class Audio contains all the listening materials in the Student's Book and is available on CD or audiocassette. The Student Self-study Audio CD contains the listening conversations and reading passages from the Student's Book.

Workbook

The **Workbook** has two pages of activities for each lesson in the Student's Book.

- The exercises are designed so learners can complete them in class or independently. Students can check their own answers with the answer key in the back of the Workbook. Workbook exercises can be assigned in class, for homework, or as student support when a class is missed.
- Grammar charts at the back of the Workbook allow students to use the Workbook for self-study.
- If used in class, the Workbook can extend classroom instructional time by 30 minutes per lesson.

Add Ventures

Add Ventures is a book of reproducible worksheets designed for use in multilevel classrooms. The worksheets give students 15–30 minutes additional practice with each lesson and can be used with homogeneous or heterogeneous groupings. These

---

[1] The Secretary's Commission on Achieving Necessary Skills, which produced a document that identifies skills for success in the workplace. For more information, see wdr.doleta.gov/SCANS.

worksheets can also be used as targeted homework practice at the level of individual students, ensuring learner success.

There are three tiered worksheets for each lesson.

- **Tier 1 Worksheets** provide additional practice for those who are at a level slightly below the Student's Book or who require more controlled practice.
- **Tier 2 Worksheets** provide additional practice for those who are on the level of the Student's Book.
- **Tier 3 Worksheets** provide additional practice that gradually expands beyond the Student's Book.

These multilevel worksheets are all keyed to the same answers for ease of classroom management.

Unit organization

Within each unit there are six lessons:

LESSON A Get ready The opening lesson focuses students on the topic of the unit. The initial exercise, *Talk about the pictures*, involves several "big" pictures. The visuals create student interest in the topic and activate prior knowledge. They help the teacher assess what learners already know and serve as a prompt for the key vocabulary of each unit. Next is *Listening*, which is based on an extended conversation. The accompanying exercises give learners the opportunity to relate the spoken and written forms of new theme-related vocabulary and to practice summarizing skills. The lesson concludes with an opportunity for students to practice language related to the theme in a communicative activity.

LESSONS B and C focus on grammar. The sections move from a *Grammar focus* that presents the grammar point in chart form; to *Practice* exercises that check comprehension of the grammar point and provide guided practice; and, finally, to *Communicate* exercises that guide learners as they generate original answers and conversations. The sections on these pages are sometimes accompanied by a *Useful language* note, which provides explanations or expressions that can be used interchangeably to accomplish a specific language function.

LESSON D Reading develops reading skills and expands vocabulary. The lesson opens with a *Before you read* exercise, whose purpose is to activate prior knowledge and encourage learners to make predictions. A *Reading tip*, which focuses learners on a specific reading skill, accompanies the *Read*

exercise. The reading section of the lesson concludes with *After you read* exercises that check students' understanding. In the Basic Student's Book and Student's Books 1 and 2, the vocabulary expansion portion of the lesson is a *Picture dictionary*. It includes a *word bank*, pictures to identify, and a conversation for practicing the new words. The words are intended to expand vocabulary related to the unit topic. In Student's Books 3 and 4, the vocabulary expansion portion of the lesson occurs in the *After you read* exercises. These exercises build awareness of word families, connotations, compound words, parts of speech, and other vocabulary expansion activities.

LESSON E Writing provides writing practice within the context of the unit. There are three kinds of exercises in the lesson: prewriting, writing, and postwriting. *Before you write* exercises provide warm-up activities to activate the language students will need for the writing and one or more exercises that provide a model for students to follow when they write. A *Writing tip*, which presents information about punctuation or organization directly related to the writing assignment, accompanies the *Write* exercise. The *Write* exercise sets goals for the student writing. In the *After you write* exercise, students share with a partner using guided questions and the steps of the writing process.

LESSON F Another view has three sections.

- **Life-skills reading** develops the scanning and skimming skills that are used with documents such as forms, charts, schedules, announcements, and ads. Multiple-choice questions that follow the document develop test-taking skills similar to CASAS[2] and BEST.[3] This section concludes with an exercise that encourages student communication by providing questions that focus on some aspect of information in the document.
- **Fun with language** provides exercises that review and sometimes expand the topic, vocabulary, or grammar of the unit. They are interactive activities for partner or group work.
- **Wrap up** refers students to the self-assessment page in the back of the book, where they can check their knowledge and evaluate their progress.

The Author Team
Gretchen Bitterlin   Sylvia Ramirez
Dennis Johnson   K. Lynn Savage
Donna Price

---

[2] The Comprehensive Adult Student Assessment System. For more information, see www.casas.org.
[3] The Basic English Skills Test. For more information, see www.cal.org/BEST.

Correlations

UNIT / PAGES	CASAS	EFF
Unit 1 **Personal information** pages 6–17	0.1.2, 0.1.4, 0.1.5, 0.1.6, 0.2.1, 0.2.4, 4.1.7, 4.6.1, 4.8.1, 4.8.2, 6.0.1, 7.1.1, 7.1.4, 7.2.1, 7.2.3, 7.2.4, 7.4.1, 7.5.1	Most EFF standards are met, with particular focus on: • Conveying ideas in writing • Cooperating with others • Listening actively • Reading with understanding • Speaking so others can understand • Taking responsibility for learning • Understanding and working with pictures
Unit 2 **At school** pages 18–29	0.1.2, 0.1.4, 0.1.5, 0.2.1, 0.2.4, 2.3.1, 2.3.2, 4.6.1, 4.8.1, 4.8.2, 6.0.1, 7.1.1, 7.1.2, 7.1.3, 7.1.4, 7.2.1, 7.2.2, 7.2.4, 7.2.6, 7.3.1, 7.3.2, 7.3.4, 7.4.1, 7.4.2, 7.5.1, 7.5.6	Most EFF standards are met, with particular focus on: • Attending to oral information • Guiding others • Monitoring comprehension and adjusting reading strategies • Paying attention to conventions of spoken English • Solving problems
Unit 3 **Friends and family** pages 32–43	0.1.2, 0.1.3, 0.1.4, 0.1.5, 0.2.1, 0.2.3, 0.2.4, 1.4.1, 1.4.7, 1.7.4, 2.3.1, 2.3.2, 3.4.2, 4.8.1, 4.8.2, 4.8.4, 5.3.7, 5.6.1, 5.6.2, 6.0.1, 7.1.4, 7.2.1, 7.4.2, 7.5.1, 8.2.6, 8.3.2	Most EFF standards are met, with particular focus on: • Organizing and presenting information to serve the purpose, context, and audience • Paying attention to conventions of spoken English • Selecting appropriate reading strategies • Solving problems • Speaking so others can understand • Testing out new learning in real-life applications
Unit 4 **Health** pages 44–55	0.1.2, 0.1.3, 0.1.5, 0.2.4, 2.3.2, 3.1.1, 3.2.1, 3.3.3, 3.4.2, 3.5.2, 3.5.4, 3.5.5, 3.5.8, 3.5.9, 4.8.1, 6.0.1, 7.1.4, 7.2.1, 7.3.2, 7.4.1, 7.4.2, 7.5.1, 8.1.1, 8.2.1	Most EFF standards are met, with particular focus on: • Attending to oral information • Conveying ideas in writing • Listening actively • Offering clear input on own interests and attitudes • Paying attention to conventions of written English • Speaking so others can understand
Unit 5 **Around town** pages 58–69	0.1.2, 0.1.4, 0.1.5, 0.2.1, 0.2.4, 2.3.1, 2.3.2, 2.6.1, 2.6.2, 2.6.3, 2.7.6, 4.8.1, 6.0.1, 7.1.1, 7.1.2, 7.1.4, 7.2.1, 7.4.2, 7.4.3, 7.5.1	Most EFF standards are met, with particular focus on: • Attending to oral information • Cooperating with others • Listening actively • Monitoring progress toward goals • Paying attention to conventions of written English • Reading with understanding • Understanding and working with pictures

SCANS	BEST Plus Form A	BEST Form B
Most SCANS standards are met, with particular focus on: • Acquiring and evaluating information • Allocating human resources • Improving basic skills • Participating as a member of a team • Practicing self-management • Teaching others	Overall test preparation is supported, with particular impact on the following items: Locator: W5 Level 1: 4.1, 4.2, 4.3 Level 3: 2.3, 4.1	Overall test preparation is supported, with particular impact on the following items: • Employment • Oral interview • Personal information • Reading passages • Writing notes
Most SCANS standards are met, with particular focus on: • Demonstrating individual responsibility • Interpreting and communicating information • Knowing how to learn • Participating as a member of a team • Practicing self-management • Solving problems	Overall test preparation is supported, with particular impact on the following items: Locator: W3 Level 2: 4.2 Level 3: 5.2	Overall test preparation is supported, with particular impact on the following items: • Oral interview • Personal information • Reading passages • Writing notes
Most SCANS standards are met, with particular focus on: • Demonstrating integrity • Improving basic skills • Organizing and maintaining information • Participating as a member of a team • Reasoning • Teaching others	Overall test preparation is supported, with particular impact on the following items: Locator: W2, W4 Level 1: 2.3 Level 2: 5, 5.1, 5.2 Level 3: 2, 2.2	Overall test preparation is supported, with particular impact on the following items: • Emergencies and safety • Housing • Oral interview • Personal information • Reading signs, ads, and notices • Time/Numbers • Writing notes
Most SCANS standards are met, with particular focus on: • Acquiring and evaluating information • Demonstrating individual responsibility • Practicing self-management • Solving problems • Teaching others	Overall test preparation is supported, with particular impact on the following items: Level 3: 1, 1.2, 1.3	Overall test preparation is supported, with particular impact on the following items: • Health and parts of the body • Numbers • Oral interview • Personal information • Reading passages • Writing notes
Most SCANS standards are met, with particular focus on: • Demonstrating sociability • Improving basic skills • Interpreting and communicating information • Knowing how to learn • Solving problems	Overall test preparation is supported, with particular impact on the following items: Level 1: 4, 4.1, 4.2 Level 3: 4, 4.1, 4.2	Overall test preparation is supported, with particular impact on the following items: • Calendar • Oral interview • Personal information • Reading passages • Reading signs, ads, and notices • Time/Numbers • Writing notes

UNIT/PAGES	CASAS	EFF
Unit 6 **Time** pages 70–81	0.1.2, 0.1.4, 0.1.5, 0.2.1, 0.2.4, 1.1.3, 2.3.1, 2.7.2, 2.7.3, 4.1.7, 4.4.1, 4.4.3, 4.4.5, 4.8.1, 6.0.1, 6.7.4, 7.1.1, 7.1.2, 7.1.4, 7.2.1, 7.2.3, 7.2.4, 7.3.2, 7.4.1, 7.4.2, 7.4.8, 7.5.1	Most EFF standards are met, with particular focus on: • Conveying ideas in writing • Cooperating with others • Listening actively • Reading with understanding • Solving problems • Speaking so others can understand
Unit 7 **Shopping** pages 84–95	0.1.2, 0.1.3, 0.1.5, 0.1.6, 0.2.1, 1.1.6, 1.2.1, 1.2.2, 1.2.5, 1.3.1, 1.4.1, 1.8.2, 4.8.1, 6.0.1, 6.5.1, 7.1.1, 7.1.4, 7.2.1, 7.2.3, 7.2.6, 7.3.1, 7.3.2, 7.4.2, 7.5.1, 7.5.5	Most EFF standards are met, with particular focus on: • Attending to oral information • Guiding others • Monitoring comprehension and adjusting reading strategies • Paying attention to conventions of written English • Selecting an alternative that is most appropriate to goal, context, and available resources • Understanding and working with pictures and numbers
Unit 8 **Work** pages 96–107	0.0.1, 0.1.2, 0.1.3, 0.1.4, 0.1.5, 0.2.1, 2.3.1, 2.3.2, 2.4.1, 4.1.2, 4.1.5, 4.1.6, 4.1.7, 4.1.8, 4.4.3, 4.5.1, 4.6.1, 4.6.2, 4.8.1, 4.8.2, 6.0.1, 7.1.1, 7.1.4, 7.2.1, 7.4.1, 7.4.2, 7.4.4, 7.5.1, 7.5.2, 7.5.6	Most EFF standards are met, with particular focus on: • Anticipating and identifying problems • Conveying ideas in writing • Listening actively • Monitoring comprehension and adjusting reading strategies • Seeking input from others in order to understand their actions and reaction • Speaking so others can understand • Testing out new learning in real-life applications
Unit 9 **Daily living** pages 110–121	0.1.2, 0.1.4, 0.1.5, 0.2.1, 0.2.4, 1.4.1, 2.3.1, 2.5.1, 2.7.3, 3.4.2, 4.8.1, 5.3.7, 5.6.1, 5.6.2, 6.0.1, 7.1.1, 7.2.1, 7.4.2, 7.5.1, 8.3.2	Most EFF standards are met, with particular focus on: • Attending to oral information • Monitoring progress toward goals • Paying attention to conventions of written English • Reading with understanding • Reflecting and evaluating • Taking responsibility for learning • Understanding and working with pictures and numbers
Unit 10 **Leisure** pages 122–133	0.1.2, 0.1.4, 0.1.5, 0.2.1, 0.2.4, 1.2.2, 1.2.5, 2.3.1, 2.3.2, 2.3.3, 2.7.1, 4.8.1, 6.0.1, 6.5.1, 7.1.1, 7.2.1, 7.2.2, 7.2.3, 7.2.6, 7.4.1, 7.4.2, 7.5.1	Most EFF standards are met, with particular focus on: • Attending to oral information • Interacting with others in ways that are friendly, courteous, and tactful • Listening actively • Monitoring comprehension and adjusting reading strategies • Paying attention to conventions of written English • Speaking so others can understand • Taking stock of where one is

SCANS	BEST Plus Form A	BEST Form B
Most SCANS standards are met, with particular focus on: • Acquiring and evaluating information • Allocating time • Interpreting and communicating information • Participating as a member of a team • Teaching others	Overall test preparation is supported, with particular impact on the following items: Locator: W5, W6	Overall test preparation is supported, with particular impact on the following items: • Employment and training • Oral interview • Personal information • Reading passages • Reading signs, ads, and notices • Time/Numbers • Writing notes
Most SCANS standards are met, with particular focus on: • Demonstrating individual responsibility • Knowing how to learn • Organizing and maintaining information • Practicing self-management • Reasoning • Solving problems	Overall test preparation is supported, with particular impact on the following items: Level 1: 1, 1.2, 1.3 Level 3: 3, 3.1, 3.2	Overall test preparation is supported, with particular impact on the following items: • Money and shopping • Numbers • Oral interview • Personal information • Reading passages • Reading signs, ads, and notices
Most SCANS standards are met, with particular focus on: • Allocating human resources • Demonstrating individual responsibility • Improving basic skills • Interpreting and communicating information • Seeing things in the mind's eye	Overall test preparation is supported, with particular impact on the following items: Locator: W5 Level 3: 2.2, 2.3	Overall test preparation is supported, with particular impact on the following items: • Calendar • Employment and training • Envelopes • Oral interview • Personal information • Reading passages • Time/Numbers • Writing notes
Most SCANS standards are met, with particular focus on: • Acquiring and evaluating information • Improving basic skills • Organizing and maintaining information • Participating as a member of a team • Practicing self-management • Teaching others	Overall test preparation is supported, with particular impact on the following items: Locator: W2, W4, W6 Level 2: 5, 5.1 Level 3: 2, 2.1, 2.2	Overall test preparation is supported, with particular impact on the following items: • Emergencies and safety • Housing • Oral interview • Personal information • Reading passages • Time/Numbers • Writing notes
Most SCANS standards are met, with particular focus on: • Knowing how to learn • Making decisions • Participating as a member of a team • Practicing self-management • Reasoning • Seeing things in the mind's eye	Overall test preparation is supported, with particular impact on the following items: Locator: W7 Level 1: 4, 4.1, 4.2 Level 2: 2.1 Level 3: 3.1, 4, 4.1	Overall test preparation is supported, with particular impact on the following items: • Calendar • Money and shopping • Numbers • Oral interview • Personal information • Reading passages • Reading signs, ads, and notices • Writing notes

Meet the *Ventures* author team

Gretchen Bitterlin has been an ESL instructor and ESL department instructional leader with the Continuing Education Program, San Diego Community College District. She now coordinates that agency's large noncredit ESL program. She was also an ESL Teacher Institute Trainer and Chair of the TESOL Task Force on Adult Education Program Standards. She is a co-author of *English for Adult Competency*.

Dennis Johnson has been an ESL instructor at City College of San Francisco, teaching all levels of ESL, since 1977. As ESL Site Coordinator, he has provided guidance to faculty in selecting textbooks. He is the author of *Get Up and Go* and co-author of *The Immigrant Experience*.

Donna Price is Associate Professor of ESL and Vocational ESL/Technology Resource Instructor for the Continuing Education Program, San Diego Community College District. She has taught all levels of ESL for 20 years and is a former recipient of the TESOL Newbury House Award for Excellence in Teaching. She is also the author of *Skills for Success*.

Sylvia Ramirez is a professor at MiraCosta College, where she coordinates the large noncredit ESL program. She has more than 30 years of experience in adult ESL, including multilevel ESL, vocational ESL, family literacy, and distance learning. She has represented the California State Department of Education in providing technical assistance to local ESL programs.

K. Lynn Savage, Series Editor, is a retired ESL teacher and Vocational ESL Resource teacher from City College of San Francisco, who trains teachers for adult education programs around the country. She chaired the committee that developed *ESL Model Standards for Adult Education Programs* (California, 1992) and is the author, co-author, and editor of many ESL materials including *Teacher Training through Video*, *Parenting for Academic Success: A Curriculum for Families Learning English*, *Crossroads Café*, *Building Life Skills*, *Picture Stories*, *May I Help You?*, and *English That Works*.

To the student

Welcome to *Ventures 3*! We want you to enjoy using your *Ventures* Student's Book in your classroom. We also hope that you will use this book to study on your own. For that reason, the Student's Book comes with an audio CD. Use it at home to review and practice the material you are learning in class. You will make faster progress in learning English if you take the time to study at home and do your homework.

Good luck in your studies!

The Author Team
Gretchen Bitterlin
Dennis Johnson
Donna Price
Sylvia Ramirez
K. Lynn Savage

Welcome

1 Meet your classmates

A Look at the picture. What do you see?

B What are the people doing?

Library hours

Mon.-Wed.
9 a.m.-9 p.m.
Thurs.-Sat.
9 a.m.-6 p.m.

September

Sun	Mon	Tue	Wed	Thurs	Fri	Sat
						1
2	3	4	5	6	7	8
9	10	11	12	13	14	15
16	17	18	19	20	21	22
23	24	25	26	27	28	29
0						

English classes
start
Monday,
September 17.

Return
books
here.

C-D

A-B

2 Introductions

A Read the answers. Write the questions.

1. *A* Where _are you from_ ?
   B I'm from Taipei, Taiwan.

2. *A* What _____ there?
   B I was a housewife.

3. *A* When _____ here?
   B I moved here in March 2006.

4. *A* Where _____ ?
   B I live in Monterey Park.

5. *A* How long _____ to get
   to school?
   B It takes me about 30 minutes to get to school.

6. *A* Are _____ ?
   B Yes, I'm married.

7. *A* What _____ next year?
   B I'll look for a job.

Listen and check your answers.

B Talk with a partner. Ask and answer questions from Exercise A about your partner.

> *A* Where are you from?
> *B* I'm from Taipei, Taiwan.

Write sentences about your partner.

My partner's name: _Liana Wang_

1. _Liana is from Taipei, Taiwan._
2. _____
3. _____
4. _____
5. _____
6. _____
7. _____

C Introduce your partner to the class.

> My partner's name is Liana Wang. She's from Taipei, Taiwan. She was a housewife there.

3 Verb tense review

A **Listen** to each sentence. Check (✓) the correct column.

	Past	Present continuous	Present	Future
1.	✓			
2.				
3.				
4.				
5.				
6.				

Listen again. Check your answers.

B **Read.** Complete the story. Use the correct verb form.

Oksana Petrova ___was___ born in Russia. She _____ a

         1. be   2. have

very good job there. She _____ a teacher.

                            3. be

In 2005, Oksana _____ Russia and _____

                     4. leave   5. move

to the United States. In 2006, she _____ a job as a

                          6. start

teacher's assistant, and she is still working there now. She usually

_____ five days a week.

    7. work

Oksana _____ to become a teacher in the U.S.

             8. want

She _____ English at night now. Next year, she

       9. study

_____ to a university. With hard work and good luck,

    10. go

Oksana _____ in four years.

      11. graduate

Listen and check your answers.

C **Talk** with a partner about work experiences. Ask and answer questions.

Before	Now	Future
Did you have a job before? Where did you work?	Do you have a job now? Where do you work?	What job would you like to have in the future?

4 Goals

A Read. Complete the sentences.

Silvia's Goal

Silvia ___wants to open___ her own beauty salon someday. To reach
          1. want / open

her goal, she _____ three steps. First, she _____
         2. need / take   3. need / go

to beauty school for two years. Second, she _____ an
                                      4. need / take

exam to get her license. Third, she _____ in a salon to get
                            5. need / work

experience. Silvia hopes to become a business owner in five years. She

_____ for anyone else.
6. not want / work

SELF-STUDY
AUDIO CD

Listen and check your answers.

B Talk with a partner. Talk about Vinh and Sofiya.

	Wants to	Needs to
Vinh	open a restaurant	1. learn how to cook 2. take business classes 3. work in a restaurant
Sofiya	get a GED	1. improve her English 2. go to night school 3. take the GED test

> Vinh wants to open a restaurant. First, he needs to learn how to cook. Second, he needs to . . .

C Talk with a partner. Ask and answer questions about goals.
Complete the chart.

> **A** What do you want to do?
> **B** I want to . . .

> **A** What steps do you need to take?
> **B** First, I need to . . .

My partner	Wants to	Needs to
		1. 2. 3.

Share information with your classmates.

Personal information

1 Talk about the pictures

A What do you see?
B What is happening?
C What's the story?

Club Havana

Fernando

Danny

2 Listening

SELF-STUDY AUDIO CD **A** **Listen** and answer the questions.

1. Who are the speakers?
2. What are they talking about?

SELF-STUDY AUDIO CD **B** **Listen again.** Put a check (✓) under the correct name.

	Fernando	Danny
1. likes dancing	✓	
2. likes staying home		
3. went out with his girlfriend		
4. is outgoing		
5. is shy		
6. wants a girlfriend		

Listen again. Check your answers.

SELF-STUDY AUDIO CD **C** **Read.** Complete the story. Listen and check your answers.

alone	dislikes	going out	party animal
dance club	enjoys	outgoing	shy

> Fernando and Danny are talking about their weekend. Fernando is a
> very friendly and ___outgoing___ person. He _____ dancing. Last
>   1   2
> night, he went to a _____ and stayed until 1:30 in the morning.
>   3
> Danny thinks Fernando is a _____ .
>   4
> Danny is different from Fernando. He is _____ and quiet. He
>   5
> _____ dancing. Danny was home _____ the whole
>   6   7
> weekend. He likes staying at home more than _____ . He wants
>   8
> a girlfriend who likes staying home, too.

D **Talk** with a partner. Ask and answer the questions.

1. What are some things you enjoy doing on the weekend?
2. Are you outgoing or shy? Give some examples.

Verbs + gerunds

1 Grammar focus: questions and statements

Questions

Do you enjoy dancing?
Does he like staying home?

Short answers

Yes, I do.
No, he doesn't.

Statements

I love dancing.
He hates staying home.

Negatives

He doesn't like dancing.
I don't mind staying home.

Gerunds often follow these verbs:

dislike	hate	love
enjoy	like	mind

For a complete grammar chart and explanation, turn to page 146.
For a list of verbs that gerunds often follow, turn to page 146.

Useful language

I don't mind means *It's OK with me.*
It doesn't bother me.

2 Practice

A Write. Complete the sentences. Use gerunds.

be	get	listen	play
do	go	pay	shop

1. Does Katrina like _____*shopping*_____ for clothes online?

2. My brother enjoys _____ soccer.

3. Mrs. Tanaka doesn't mind _____ up early.

4. I love _____ to the birds in the morning.

5. Do you mind _____ to the movies by yourself?

6. Do you enjoy _____ alone?

7. Most people don't enjoy _____ bills every month.

8. Winston dislikes _____ English homework.

Listen and check your answers.

B **Talk** with a partner. Ask and answer questions about the pictures.

> *A* Does Rita love playing cards?
> *B* Yes, she does. She loves playing cards with friends.

> *A* Does Karl enjoy taking out the garbage?
> *B* No, he doesn't. He doesn't enjoy taking out the garbage at all.

Rita

love / play cards with friends

Karl

enjoy / take out the garbage

Ramon

like / go to the beach

Kim

mind / stand in line

Nasim

dislike / work out

Liz and Fred

hate / work in the garden

Write a sentence about each picture.

Rita loves playing cards with friends.

3 Communicate

A **Work** in a small group. Ask and answer questions about the activities.

> *A* Tam, do you like being alone?
> *B* I don't mind it. What about you?

- be alone
- dance
- learn languages

- surf the Internet
- play sports
- read magazines

- talk on the phone
- exercise
- clean the house

B **Share** information about your classmates.

> **Useful language**
> Say *What about you?* OR *How about you?* to ask someone the same question they asked you.

Comparisons

1 Grammar focus: *more than, less than, as much as*

Statements

I enjoy walking more than driving.
She likes cooking less than eating.
They enjoy singing as much as dancing.

For a grammar explanation, turn to page 152.

2 Practice

A **Write.** Complete the sentences. Use *more than*, *less than*, or *as much as*.

1. Sally enjoys cooking ___more than___ washing dishes.

2. Alfredo loves listening to music _____ playing an instrument.

3. Pam likes working _____ going to school.

4. Marta enjoys painting _____ jogging.

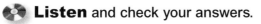 **Listen** and check your answers.

B **Work** with a partner. Talk about the bar graph. Use *more than*, *less than*, and *as much as*.

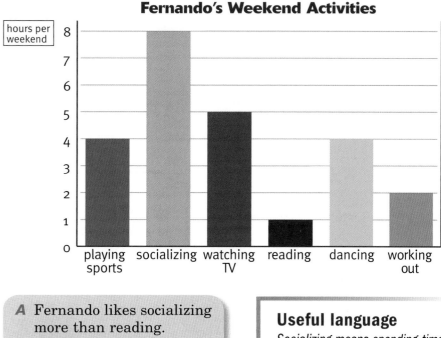

Fernando's Weekend Activities

A Fernando likes socializing
more than reading.
B That's right.

Useful language
Socializing means *spending time
with friends or family.*

1. socializing / reading
2. playing sports / dancing
3. socializing / working out
4. watching TV / socializing
5. reading / playing sports
6. working out / reading

Write sentences about Fernando's weekend activities.

Fernando enjoys socializing more than reading.

3 Communicate

A **Work** in a small group. Ask and answer questions about the activities
in Exercise 2B.

Which do you like more, playing
sports or socializing?

I like socializing more
than playing sports.

B **Share** information about your classmates.

Amelia likes socializing more
than playing sports.

1 Before you read

Look at the reading tip. Answer the questions.

1. What jobs do the people in the pictures have?
2. What kind of person probably enjoys doing each job?
3. What do you predict this reading is about?

2 Read

SELF-STUDY AUDIO CD **Read** the magazine article. Listen and read again.

> Before you read, look at the title and the pictures. Predict, or guess, what you are going to read about. This will help you to read faster.

Your Personality and Your JOB

What is the perfect job for you? It depends a lot on your personality. People think, act, and feel in different ways, and there are interesting jobs for every kind of person. Three common personality types are outgoing, intellectual, and creative.

Outgoing people enjoy meeting others and helping them. They are good talkers. They are friendly, and they get along well with other people. They often become nurses, counselors, teachers, or social workers.

Intellectual people like thinking about problems and finding answers to hard questions. They often enjoy reading and playing games like chess. Many intellectual people like working alone more than working in a group. They may become scientists, computer programmers, or writers.

Creative people enjoy making things. They like to imagine things that are new and different. Many of them become artists such as painters, dancers, or musicians. Architects, designers, and photographers are other examples of creative jobs.

Before you choose a career, think about your personality type. If you want to be happy in your work, choose the right job for your personality.

3 After you read

A Check your understanding.

1. What do outgoing people enjoy doing? What jobs are good for them?
2. What do intellectual people like? What jobs are good for them?
3. What do creative people enjoy? What jobs are good for them?
4. Why is it important for you to know your personality type?

B Build your vocabulary.

1. Find these words in the reading, and underline them.

personality   intellectual
type   creative
outgoing   artists

2. Find these phrases in the reading, and circle them.

enjoy meeting others

like to imagine things that are new and different

like thinking about problems

think, act, and feel in different ways

painters, dancers, or musicians

every kind of person

3. Look at the phrases in Exercise B2. They are clues to help you guess the meaning of these words. Write the clues under the words.

1. personality

_____

2. type

_____

3. outgoing

_____

4. intellectual

_____

5. creative

_____

6. artists

_____

4. Match the words and the definitions.

1. personality _____
2. type _____
3. outgoing _____
4. intellectual _____
5. creative _____
6. artist _____

a. a kind of person or thing
b. good at making things that are new and different
c. enjoys thinking and finding answers
d. a person who paints, dances, writes, or draws
e. the natural way a person thinks, feels, and acts
f. friendly

C Talk with a partner. Ask and answer the questions.

1. What personality type are you? Why do you think so?
2. What is a good job for you?

1 Before you write

A Talk with a partner. Look at the pictures. Answer the questions.

1. What are these people doing? What are their jobs?
2. Do you think these people are outgoing? intellectual? creative?
3. Adjectives are words that describe things. For example, *outgoing* is an adjective. What other adjectives describe these people?

B Work in a small group. Complete the web. Use adjectives that describe personality.

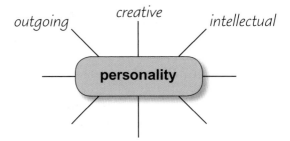

outgoing   *creative*   *intellectual*

personality

C Read the paragraph.

Marcos
September 9

The Right Job

My sister, Leona, has the right job for her personality. She's a nurse. She works in a big hospital in the Philippines. Leona is a very outgoing person. She's very friendly with all her patients, and she enjoys talking to everybody in the hospital. She is warm and helpful. I think a nurse is a good job for her because it fits her personality.

Work with a partner. Answer the questions.

1. What does the first sentence say about Leona?
2. What is Leona's job?
3. Where does she work?
4. Leona is an outgoing person. Which sentences explain this?
5. Which adjectives describe Leona?
6. Is a nurse a good job for Leona? Why?

To describe someone's personality, use adjectives. You can also tell what the person likes or enjoys.

2 Write

Write a paragraph about the right job for someone you know. Use Exercises 1B and 1C to help you.

3 After you write

A Check your writing.

	Yes	No
1. I included a job and personality type.	☐	☐
2. I included what the person likes or enjoys.	☐	☐
3. I included adjectives.	☐	☐

B Share your writing with a partner.

1. Take turns. Read your paragraph to a partner.
2. Comment on your partner's paragraph. Ask your partner a question about the paragraph. Tell your partner one thing you learned.

Another view

1 Life-skills reading

●○○ Loveland

Fun-loving DM (46, 5'11", beard, salt-and-pepper hair, N/S) enjoys taking motorcycle trips, camping outdoors, and spending time at the ocean. Seeking outgoing SF (40–50) for bike trips and fun.

Warm, kind, intelligent SM (27, 5'8") enjoys playing guitar, cooking, taking pictures. Seeking gentle SF (25–30) for musical evenings at home.

Caring SF (30, 5'5") loves playing tennis. Seeking good-looking, honest, active SM (28–35) with a good heart to share life together.

Useful language

DM = divorced male
N/S = nonsmoker
SF = single female
SM = single male

A **Read** the questions. Look at the Web page. Circle the answers.

1. How tall is the man on the motorcycle?
   a. under 5 feet
   b. 5 feet 2 inches
   c. 5 feet 11 inches
   d. over 6 feet

2. What word describes the younger man?
   a. friendly
   b. fun-loving
   c. honest
   d. kind

3. What does the woman enjoy doing?
   a. playing guitar
   b. playing tennis
   c. taking motorcycle trips
   d. none of the above

4. Which ad talks about evenings at home?
   a. the first ad
   b. the second ad
   c. the third ad
   d. all of the above

B **Talk** with your classmates. Ask and answer the questions.

Is the Internet a good place to find a new friend? Why or why not?

2 Fun with language

A Talk with your classmates. Complete the chart.

Elsa, do you love dancing?

Yes, I do.

Find someone who:	Name
loves dancing	*Elsa*
doesn't mind working alone	
enjoys going to parties more than staying home	
dislikes reading	
likes painting	
enjoys camping	
loves having pets	
loves playing guitar	

Share information about your classmates.

Elsa loves dancing.

B Play a game.
Write your own personal ad on a card.
Don't write your name.
Give your card to your teacher.
Your teacher will read each card out loud.
The class will guess who wrote the ad.

3 Wrap up

Complete the **Self-assessment** on page 141.

Get ready

1 Talk about the pictures

A What do you see?
B What is happening?
C What's the story?

At school

2 Listening

SELF-STUDY
AUDIO CD **A** 💿 **Listen** and answer the questions.

1. Who are the speakers?
2. What are they talking about?

SELF-STUDY
AUDIO CD **B** 💿 **Listen again.** Put a check (✓) next to Alex's study problems.

1. ☑ too many things to do   4. ☐ can't pronounce English words
2. ☐ always late for school   5. ☐ can't remember vocabulary
3. ☐ can't concentrate   6. ☐ can't speak English well

Listen again. Check your answers.

SELF-STUDY
AUDIO CD **C** 💿 **Read.** Complete the story. Listen and check your answers.

active	concentrate	index cards	paper
boring	discouraged	list	underline

Alex has been at the library for more than two hours, and he is very ___discouraged___ [1]. He has many things to do. He needs to study for a test and write a _____ [2]. He needs to finish reading a book, but he can't _____ [3]. He says the book is _____ [4].

Alex's friend Bella gives him some study advice. First, she tells Alex to make a _____ [5] of all the things he needs to do. Next, she says he has to be a more _____ [6] reader. For example, he should _____ [7] main ideas in his textbooks. Finally, she tells him to write vocabulary words on _____ [8] and study them when he has free time.

With Bella's help, Alex plans to study smarter, not harder.

D **Talk** with a partner. Ask and answer the questions.

1. What study problems do you have?
2. What can you do to study better?

Lesson B *Present perfect*

1 Grammar focus: questions with *How long*; *for* and *since*

Questions

How long has **Alex** been **here**?
How long have **you** known **Alex**?

Answers

He has been **here** for two years.
I have known **him** since January.

Past participles		Time phrases	
Regular verbs	**Irregular verbs**	for two hours	since 6:00 p.m.
live → lived	be → been	for one year	since February
study → studied	have → had	for five months	since last year
work → worked	know → known		
	speak → spoken		
	teach → taught		

For a complete grammar chart and explanation, turn to page 148.
For a list of irregular verbs, turn to page 151.

2 Practice

A Write. Complete the sentences. Use the present perfect.

1. **A** How long ___*has*___ Manya _____*been*_____ in the computer lab?
    (be)
   B Since six o'clock.

2. **A** How long _____ Avi _____ Bella?
    (know)
   B For four months.

3. **A** How long _____ Kayla _____ at the library?
    (work)
   B Since September.

4. **A** How long _____ Mrs. Bateson _____ at the
    (teach)
   adult school?
   B For 20 years.

5. **A** How long _____ you _____ in Canada?
    (live)
   B For one year.

6. **A** How long _____ Omar _____ two jobs?
    (have)
   B Since last year.

Listen and check your answers. Then practice with a partner.

B **Talk** with a partner. Ask and answer questions about Alex. Use *since*.

> *A* How long has Alex been in the United States?
> *B* Since January 2006.

Alex's Recent History

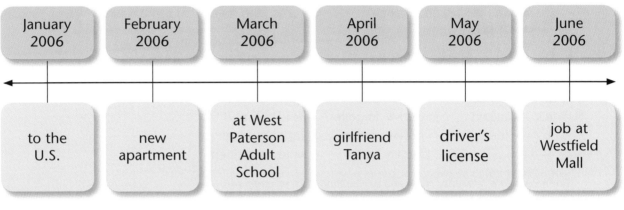

January 2006	February 2006	March 2006	April 2006	May 2006	June 2006
to the U.S.	new apartment	at West Paterson Adult School	girlfriend Tanya	driver's license	job at Westfield Mall

1. be in the U.S.
2. live in his apartment
3. study at West Paterson Adult School
4. know Tanya
5. have a driver's license
6. work at Westfield Mall

Write today's date. Then write sentences about Alex. Use *for*.

Today is July 23, 2009.
Alex has been in the U.S. for three years and six months.

3 Communicate

A **Work** in a small group. Ask and answer questions with *How long*.

> *A* How long have you studied English?
> *B* For three years. / Since 2004.
> *A* That's interesting.

1. study / English
2. live / in this country
3. be / at this school
4. work / in this country
5. have / your job
6. know / our teacher
7. be / married
8. lived / in your present home

Useful language
To express interest or surprise, you can say:
That's interesting.
Really?
Wow!

B **Share** information about your classmates.

Present perfect

1 Grammar focus: questions with *ever*; short answers

Questions

Have you ever talked to a counselor?
Has Sonia ever studied French?

Short answers

Yes, I have.	No, I haven't.
Yes, she has.	No, she hasn't.

Past participles

Regular verbs

ask → asked
talk → talked
try → tried

Irregular verbs

do → done	make → made
forget → forgotten	read → read
get → gotten	take → taken
lose → lost	write → written

For a complete grammar chart and explanation, turn to page 148.
For a list of irregular verbs, turn to page 151.

2 Practice

A Write. Complete the sentences. Use *ever*.

1. **A** ___Has Laura ever talked___ to her school counselor?
   (Laura / talk)
   B No, she hasn't.

2. **A** _____ your teacher's name?
   (you / forget)
   B Yes, I have.

3. **A** _____ a book in English?
   (Joseph / read)
   B No, he hasn't. But he wants to.

4. **A** _____ late to school?
   (Mary and Paula / be)
   B No, they haven't.

5. **A** _____ to speak English with your neighbors?
   (you / try)
   B Yes, I have.

6. **A** _____ the wrong bus to school?
   (he / take)
   B No, he hasn't.

Listen and check your answers. Then practice with a partner.

B **Talk** with a partner. Ask and answer questions about study habits.

> **A** Have you ever made a to-do list?
> **B** No, I haven't.
> **A** Have you ever asked questions in class?
> **B** Yes, I have.

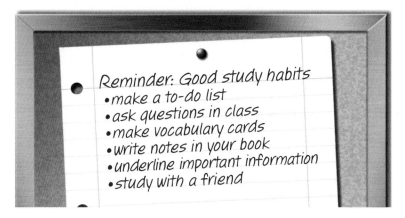

Reminder: Good study habits
- make a to-do list
- ask questions in class
- make vocabulary cards
- write notes in your book
- underline important information
- study with a friend

Write sentences about your partner.

Omar hasn't ever made a to-do list. He has asked questions in class.

3 Communicate

A **Work** in a small group. Ask and answer questions about study problems. Complete the chart.

> **A** Have you ever had trouble concentrating?
> **B** Yes, I have.

Study problems	Name	Name
have trouble concentrating		
forget to study for a test		
lose your textbook		
do the wrong homework		
be late to school		
(your idea)		

B **Share** information about your classmates. Give advice.

> Ana has had trouble concentrating.

> She should do her homework in a quiet place.

1 Before you read

Talk with your classmates. Answer the questions.

1. What is the reading about?
2. What are *strategies*?
3. How many strategies are there? What are they?

2 Read

SELF-STUDY
AUDIO CD **Read** the article from a student magazine. Listen and read again.

Strategies for Learning English

Have you ever felt discouraged because it's hard to speak and understand English? Don't give up! Here are three strategies to help you learn faster and remember more.

Strategy #1 Set goals.

Have you ever set goals for learning English? When you set goals, you decide what you want to learn. Then you make a plan to help you reach your goals. Maybe your goal is to learn more vocabulary. There are many ways to do this. For example, you can read in English for 15 minutes every day. You can also learn one new word every day.

Strategy #2 Look for opportunities to practice English.

Talk to everyone. Speak with people in the store, at work, and in the park. Don't worry about making mistakes. And don't forget to ask questions. For example, if your teacher uses a word you don't understand, ask a question like "What does that word mean?"

Strategy #3 Guess.

Don't try to translate every word. When you read, concentrate on clues such as pictures or other words in the sentence to help you understand. You can also make guesses when you are talking to people. For example, look at their faces and hand gestures – the way they move their hands – to help you guess the meaning.

Set goals, look for opportunities to practice, and guess. Do these things every day, and you will learn more English!

In a reading, *for example* means *details will follow*.

3 After you read

A Check your understanding.

1. What are *goals*?
2. What is an example of setting goals?
3. What is an example of looking for opportunities to practice English?
4. You ask someone in line at a supermarket, "What time is it?" What strategy are you using?
5. If you read a story without using a dictionary, what strategy are you using?

B Build your vocabulary.

1. Look at the chart. Find the vocabulary words in the reading. Underline them.

2. Use the context to decide the part of speech of each word – *noun* or *verb*. Write it in the chart.

3. Circle the best definition to match the part of speech.

Vocabulary	Part of speech	Definition
1. set	*verb*	a. a group of related things, such as dishes (b.) to choose or decide on something, such as a goal
2. plan		a. something you have decided to do b. to decide about something you want to do
3. practice		a. an activity you do to improve your ability b. to do something regularly to improve your ability
4. guess		a. an answer that you think is right, but you're not sure b. to give an answer that you think is right
5. clues		a. information you use to guess or solve problems b. to give someone useful information
6. pictures		a. paintings, drawings, or photographs b. to imagine something
7. gestures		a. hand movements that have a special meaning b. to tell something by moving your hands

C Talk with a partner. Ask and answer the questions.

1. Have you ever set goals for learning English? What were they?
2. How do you practice something new? Give an example.
3. When you speak, what gestures do you use?

Writing

1 Before you write

A Work in a small group. Complete the chart with examples of strategies for learning English. Use the reading on page 24 and your own ideas.

Strategy	Examples from reading	Your examples
Set goals.	*Read for 15 minutes in English every day.*	*Write in English every day for five minutes.*
Practice English.		
Guess.		

B Read the paragraph.

My Strategies for Learning English

I have read about some useful strategies for learning English. One strategy I really like is setting goals. My goal is to learn more English words. I'm going to do several things to reach this goal. For example, I'm going to learn one new English word every day. I'm also going to write my new words in a notebook. Another strategy I will try is looking for places to practice my English. For example, I'm going to talk more to English speakers at the store and at work. I can't wait to try these new strategies because I want to speak, read, and write English better.

> Use examples to support your ideas.

Work with a partner. Answer the questions.

1. How did the writer learn about the strategies?
2. What is the writer's first strategy?
3. What is the writer's goal? What is the writer going to do to reach this goal?
4. What is the second strategy? What examples does the writer give?
5. The author says, "I can't wait to try these new strategies." What does that mean?
6. Do you think these strategies could help you?

C Write a plan for a paragraph about strategies for learning English. Answer the questions.

1. What is one strategy you have wanted to try?	
2. What is one example of this strategy?	
3. What is another strategy you have wanted to try?	
4. What is one example of this strategy?	
5. Why do you want to try these strategies?	

2 Write

Write a paragraph about strategies for learning English. Write two strategies and one or two examples for each one. Use Exercises 1B and 1C to help you.

3 After you write

A Check your writing.

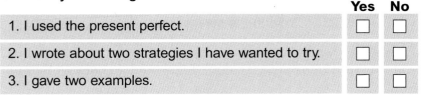

	Yes	No
1. I used the present perfect.	☐	☐
2. I wrote about two strategies I have wanted to try.	☐	☐
3. I gave two examples.	☐	☐

B Share your writing with a partner.

1. Take turns. Read your paragraph to a partner.
2. Comment on your partner's paragraph. Ask your partner a question about the paragraph. Tell your partner one thing you learned.

1 Life-skills reading

7 Tips for Taking Tests

1. Read the instructions carefully. Ask the teacher if you don't understand them.

2. Skim the whole test before you begin. This will help you decide how to use your time.

3. Answer the easiest questions first.

4. Don't spend a lot of time on one question. Go back to it later if you have time.

5. Don't worry if other classmates finish before you. Pay attention to your own test.

6. Leave time to check your answers. Make sure you have answered every question.

7. Don't look at another student's paper.

Culture note
During a test, don't look at another student's paper, ask another student for help, or help another student. These are types of cheating.

A Read the questions. Look at the tips. Circle the answers.

1. Which tip tells you to read the whole test before you answer any questions?
   a. Tip 1   c. Tip 6
   b. Tip 2   d. Tip 7

2. Which tip tells you to answer the questions you know first?
   a. Tip 1   c. Tip 3
   b. Tip 2   d. Tip 4

3. Which tip tells you to skip the questions you don't know and go back to them later?
   a. Tip 3   c. Tip 5
   b. Tip 4   d. Tip 6

4. Which tip says you should answer every question?
   a. Tip 1   c. Tip 4
   b. Tip 3   d. Tip 6

B Talk with a partner. Ask and answer the questions.

1. Have you ever tried any of these tips? Did they help you?

2. Do you have any other tips for taking tests? What are they?

2 Fun with language

A **Read** the strategies for learning English. Check (✓) the ones you use.
There are no right or wrong answers.

☐	1. I study with classmates.
☐	2. I study alone.
☐	3. I read English books, magazines, and newspapers.
☐	4. I use a dictionary.
☐	5. I watch TV in English.
☐	6. I watch English movies or DVDs.
☐	7. I speak with English speakers at work, at the store, or at school.
☐	8. I use the Internet to learn English.
☐	9. I write e-mail in English.
☐	10. I sing English songs.
☐	11. I make vocabulary cards.
☐	12. I write new words in a notebook.

Talk with a partner. Ask and answer the questions.

1. Which strategies are the same for both of you?
2. Which strategies are different?
3. Do you have other strategies for learning English? What are they?

B **Work** in a group. Look at the sayings. What do they mean?

1. Never let formal education get in the way of learning.
   —Mark Twain
2. Learning is a treasure that will follow its owner everywhere.
   —Chinese proverb
3. By learning you will teach, by teaching you will learn.
   —Latin proverb
4. Give a fish to a man; he has food for a day. Teach a man to fish;
   he learns a skill for life.
   —Chinese proverb

Share your answers with another group.

3 Wrap up

Complete the **Self-assessment** on page 141.

Review

1 Listening

Listen. Put a check (✓) under the correct name.

	Vladimir	**Marisol**
1. asks the teacher questions		✓
2. asks another student questions		
3. puts vocabulary on index cards		
4. talks to co-workers		
5. is shy		
6. is outgoing		

Talk with a partner. Check your answers.

2 Grammar

A Write. Complete the story. Use the correct words.

Homework Problems

Jameela _____*has had*_____ a lot of problems with her son, Faisal, for the past
      1. has / has had

two months. He doesn't enjoy _____ science. He _____
            2. studying / study   3. get / has gotten

bad grades on his tests. The teacher said that Faisal _____ his
                                      4. doesn't do / hasn't done

homework since December. Faisal said he hates _____ his science
                                   5. doing / do

homework because he doesn't understand it. Jameela _____ overtime
                                       6. works / has worked

at her job for the past two months, so she _____ at home to help him.
                                7. hasn't been / won't be

What should Jameela and her son do?

B Write. Look at the answers. Write the questions.

1. **A** How long _has Jameela had problems with her son_ ?

   B Jameela has had problems with her son for the past two months.

2. **A** _____ ever _____ ?

   B Yes, he has. Faisal has gotten bad grades on his tests for the past two months.

3. **A** How long _____ ?

   B Jameela has worked overtime for the past two months.

Talk with a partner. Ask and answer the questions.

3 Pronunciation: stressing content words

A 💿 **Listen** to the stressed content words in each sentence. Content words include main verbs, nouns, adverbs, adjectives, and question words.

1. She <u>loves</u> <u>playing</u> <u>cards</u> with <u>friends</u>.
2. He <u>hates</u> <u>working</u> in the <u>garden</u>.
3. Do you <u>like</u> <u>being</u> <u>alone</u>?
4. She <u>enjoys</u> <u>cooking</u> less than <u>eating</u>.
5. I <u>like</u> <u>living</u> in the <u>city</u>.
6. <u>How</u> <u>long</u> has <u>Shen</u> <u>studied</u> <u>English</u>?
7. He's been <u>here</u> for <u>six</u> <u>months</u>.
8. Have you <u>ever</u> <u>studied</u> <u>Korean</u>?

💿 **Listen again and repeat.** Stress the content words.

B 💿 **Listen and repeat.** Then underline the content words.

1. <u>What</u> is the <u>perfect</u> <u>job</u> for you?

2. The perfect job depends on your personality.

3. Have you ever felt discouraged?

4. Have you ever set goals for learning English?

5. What does that word mean?

6. Intellectual people often enjoy working alone.

Read your sentences to a partner. Compare your answers.

C **Read** the paragraph. Underline the content words.

My sister has the right job for her personality. She's a nurse. She works in a big hospital in the Philippines. She is a very outgoing person. She's very friendly with all her patients, and she enjoys talking to people in the hospital. She is warm and helpful. I think a nurse is a good job for her because it fits her personality.

Talk with a partner. Compare your answers. Read the paragraph to your partner. Stress the content words.

Get ready

1 Talk about the pictures

A What do you see?
B What is happening?
C What's the story?

Friends and family

Ana

Maria

2 Listening

A 🔊 **Listen** and answer the questions.

    1. Who are the speakers?

    2. What are they talking about?

B 🔊 **Listen again.** Put a check (✓) next to Ana's problems.

1. ☑ been busy	4. ☐ car alarm broken
2. ☐ children sick	5. ☐ smoke alarm needs battery
3. ☐ washing machine broken	6. ☐ neighbors are noisy

Listen again. Check your answers.

C 🔊 **Read.** Complete the story. Listen and check your answers.

appreciates	come over	favor	noisy
borrow	complain	noise	owe

    Ana and Maria are neighbors. Ana calls Maria because she needs a

_____*favor*_____ . The smoke alarm in Ana's kitchen is beeping. She needs
      1

to change the battery, but the ceiling in her kitchen is too high. Ana asks

to _____ Maria's ladder.
    2

    Maria says her husband, Daniel, will _____ with a ladder
                          3

and help Ana. Ana says, "I _____ you one." This means she
                      4

_____ Maria and Daniel's help, and she will do a favor for them
    5

in the future.

    Next, Maria tells Ana about their _____ neighbors. The
                              6

neighbors had a party on Saturday night. Because of the _____ ,
                                7

Maria and Daniel couldn't sleep. Ana tells Maria that

she should _____ to the apartment manager.
         8

Useful language

When you *lend* something
to someone, you give it.

When you *borrow* something
from someone, you receive it.

D **Talk** with a partner. Ask and answer the questions.

    1. Have you ever borrowed something from a neighbor?
       What did you borrow?

    2. Have you ever lent something to a neighbor? What did you lend?

Because and *because of*

1 Grammar focus: clauses and phrases

because + subject + verb	*because of* + noun phrase
Ana can't reach the smoke alarm because the ceiling is too high.	Ana can't reach the smoke alarm because of the high ceiling.
Because the ceiling is too high, Ana can't reach the smoke alarm.	Because of the high ceiling, Ana can't reach the smoke alarm.

For a grammar explanation, turn to page 152.

Useful language
When you read aloud, pause when you see a comma.
Because of the high ceiling, (pause)
Ana can't reach the smoke alarm.

2 Practice

A Write. Complete the sentences. Use *because* or *because of.*

A Nice Surprise

Lei wanted to bake a cake _____*because*_____ it was her neighbor Margy's birthday. Lei needed
1

to go to the store _____ she didn't
2

have any flour. However, her car had a flat tire.

_____ this problem, she couldn't drive to the store. She couldn't
3

walk to the store _____ the distance. It was more than a mile
4

away. Lei had a clever idea. She went to Margy and asked to borrow a cup of

flour. Margy was happy to help _____ she had a lot of flour and
5

she was a good neighbor. Two hours later, Lei returned to Margy's house with a

beautiful cake. When Margy opened the door, Lei shouted, "Happy birthday!"

Margy was very surprised and happy. _____ the nice surprise,
6

Margy had a wonderful birthday!

💿 **Listen** and check your answers.

B **Talk** with a partner. Ask and answer questions about the problems.

> **A** Why couldn't you sleep last night?
> **B** Because of my noisy neighbors.

Problem	Reason
1. You couldn't sleep last night.	noisy neighbors
2. You couldn't make a cake.	didn't have any eggs
3. The neighbors couldn't lock the door.	lock was broken
4. You couldn't change the alarm.	didn't have a ladder
5. The children couldn't play outside.	the rain
6. You couldn't come to school.	car had a flat tire

Write a sentence about each problem.

I couldn't sleep last night because of my noisy neighbors.

3 Communicate

A **Work** in a small group. Ask and answer questions. Complete the chart.

> **A** Why did you come to this country, Shakir?
> **B** Because of my children.
> **A** Why do you live in this neighborhood?
> **B** Because it's close to my job.

Name	Why did you come to this country?	Why do you live in this neighborhood?
Shakir	*his children live here*	*close to his job*

B **Share** information about your classmates.

Enough and too

1 Grammar focus: *enough* and *too* with adjectives

Adjective + *enough*

The ladder is tall enough.

It's tall enough to reach the ceiling.

***too* + adjective**

The ceiling is too high.

It's too high to reach.

not* + adjective + *enough

The woman is not tall enough.

She is not tall enough to reach the ceiling.

For a grammar explanation, turn to page 152.

Adjectives		
big	expensive	far
close	experienced	high

2 Practice

A Write. Complete the sentences. Use *enough* or *too*.

Too Far to Visit

My neighbors – the Mansours – have four children. Their house isn't big _____ . Mr. and Mrs. Mansour think

1

it's _____ expensive to live in the city. Their rent

2

is _____ high. Last weekend, the Mansours bought

3

a house outside the city. It has four bedrooms. It's big

_____ for the whole family. However, the new

4

house is _____ far from Mr. Mansour's job, so he's going to look for a new

5

job. Mr. Mansour is an experienced

engineer. He's experienced _____

6

to find a new job. I will miss the

Mansours. I probably can't visit them.

Their new house isn't close _____

7

for me to visit.

🔘 **Listen** and check your answers.

B Work with a partner. Talk about the pictures. Use *too*, *enough*, and *not . . . enough*.

> **A** It's too cold to swim.
> **B** I know. It isn't warm enough.

> **A** It's hot enough to swim.
> **B** Yes, you're right.

cold / swim / warm

hot / swim

young / drive / old

old / drive

weak / lift the TV / strong

strong / lift the TV

Write sentences about each picture.

It's too cold to swim.
It isn't warm enough to swim.

3 Communicate

Work in a small group. Talk about what you are *too young*, *too old*, *young enough*, or *old enough* to do. Give your opinions.

Useful language
I agree. = My opinion is the same as yours.
I disagree. / I don't agree. = My opinion is different from yours.

> I'm too young to get married.

> I agree. Young people should wait to get married.

Lesson D · *Reading*

1 Before you read

Look at the title and the picture. Answer the questions.

1. Have you ever heard of Neighborhood Watch? What is it?
2. Is there a Neighborhood Watch in your area?

2 Read

SELF-STUDY
AUDIO CD

Read the article from a neighborhood newsletter. Listen and read again.

> The first sentence of a paragraph usually tells the main idea. The other sentences give details. Facts and examples are types of details.

Neighborhood Watch Success Story

by Latisha Holmes, President, Rolling Hills Neighborhood Watch

People often ask me about the role of Neighborhood Watch. My answer is: Because of Neighborhood Watch, our neighborhood is safer and nicer. Members of Neighborhood Watch help each other and watch out for each other. For example, we watch out for our neighbors' houses when they aren't home. We help elderly neighbors with yard work. Once a month, we get together to paint over graffiti.

Last Wednesday, the Neighborhood Watch team had another success story. Around 8:30 p.m., members of our Neighborhood Watch were out on a walk. Near the Corner Café, they noticed two men next to George Garcia's car. George lives at 1157 Rolling Hills Drive. The men were trying to break into the car. Suddenly, the car alarm went off. The men ran away and got into a car down the street. But they weren't quick enough. Our Neighborhood Watch members wrote down the car's license plate number and called the police. Later that night, the police arrested the two men.

I would like to congratulate our Neighborhood Watch team on their good work. Because of their good work, Rolling Hills is a safer neighborhood today.

For information about Neighborhood Watch, please call 213-555-1234.

3 After you read

A Check your understanding.

1. What is the main idea of the first paragraph?
2. What are three examples of the role of Neighborhood Watch?
3. Does the second paragraph give facts or examples?
4. What did the Neighborhood Watch team see? What did they do?

B Build your vocabulary.

1. Read the dictionary entry for the word *get*. Find the definition of *get together*.

> **get** /get/ [T] **getting**, *past* **got**, *past part* **gotten**   to take (something)
>   into your possession
>   **get together** *v/adv* [I/T] to meet; to have a meeting or party

2. *Get together* is a two-word verb. Look at the article in Exercise 2. Match the two-word verbs.

get	watch	break	run	get	go
into	out (for)	together	into	away	off

3. Write each verb in Exercise B2 next to its definition.

1. to meet	*get together*
2. to enter (a car legally)	
3. to enter (a car illegally)	
4. to make a sudden, loud noise	
5. to escape; to leave a place very fast	
6. to take care of	

4. Complete the sentences with the verbs in Exercise B3.

a. Let's ___*get together*___ for coffee tomorrow, OK?

b. Somebody tried to _____ my neighbor's house.

c. I saw the girl next door _____ a car and drive away.

d. My cats always _____ when the door is open.

e. My neighbor's car alarm _____ at 3:00 a.m. every morning.

f. All the people on my street _____ for each other's children.

C Talk with a partner. Ask and answer the questions.

1. Do you enjoy getting together with friends? What do you do?
2. Do you and your neighbors watch out for each other? How?

Writing

1 Before you write

A Talk with a partner. Answer the questions.

1. Have you ever complained to your landlord or apartment manager?
2. What was the problem?
3. How did you complain – in person, by telephone, or in writing?
4. What happened?

B Read the letter of complaint.

January 14, 2009

Acme Properties
100 25th Avenue
New York, NY 10011

To Whom It May Concern:

My name is Luis Ramos. I live at 156 South Flower Street, Apartment 3. I am writing because my neighbors in Apartment 9 are too noisy. I asked them to be quiet, but they still have loud parties almost every night. Because of the noise, my children can't sleep.

Can you please tell them to be quiet? I hope you will take care of this as soon as possible.

Thank you in advance.

Sincerely,

Luis Ramos
Luis Ramos

> **Culture note**
> When you don't know the name of the person you are writing to, use *To Whom It May Concern.*

Work with a partner. Answer the questions.

1. What is the date of the letter?
2. Who is the letter to?
3. Does the writer know the person's name?
4. Who wrote the letter?
5. What is the problem?
6. What does the writer want the manager to do?

C Complete the letter of complaint.

advance	because of	soon
because	sincerely	too

To Whom It May Concern:

My name is Alina Krasinski. I live at 156 South Flower Street,
Apartment 6. I am writing ___*because*___ the pipes under my kitchen
$\quad\quad\quad\quad\quad\quad\quad\quad\quad\quad$ 1
sink are leaking. _____ the leak, my water bill will be _____
$\quad\quad\quad\quad\quad\quad$ 2 $\quad\quad\quad\quad\quad\quad\quad\quad\quad\quad\quad\quad\quad\quad\quad\quad\quad$ 3
high next month. The water is also bad for the kitchen floor.

Can you please come as _____ as possible to fix the leak?
$\quad\quad\quad\quad\quad\quad\quad\quad\quad\quad\quad\quad\quad\quad$ 4

Thank you in _____ .
$\quad\quad\quad\quad\quad\quad\quad\quad\quad$ 5

_____ ,
$\quad\quad$ 6

Alina Krasinski
Alina Krasinski

A letter of complaint should include:
• the problem
• examples
• a request to fix the problem

D Talk with your classmates. What housing problems
do people complain about?

2 Write

Write a letter of complaint. Use the letters in Exercises 1B and 1C to help you.

3 After you write

A Check your writing.

	Yes	No
1. I used *To Whom It May Concern* or the person's name.	☐	☐
2. I included the problem and an example.	☐	☐
3. I included a request to fix the problem.	☐	☐

B Share your writing with a partner.

1. Take turns. Read your letter to a partner.
2. Comment on your partner's letter. Ask your partner a question
   about the letter. Tell your partner one thing you learned.

Another view

1 Life-skills reading

Community Center Volunteers Needed

Organization:	Oak Park Community Center
Volunteers needed:	10
Date:	Open
Time:	9:00 a.m.–10:00 p.m.
Estimated time:	4 hours per day
Location:	15 Franklin Street San Diego, CA 92111
Description:	**1.** Volunteers to provide food and drinks to visitors **2.** Volunteers for theater to greet people, answer questions, assist with seating **3.** Volunteers for Arts Program to assist teachers with classes
Requirements:	Reliable; teamwork skills; good customer service Prefer 18 years old and over

A Read the questions. Look at the ad. Circle the answers.

1. How many volunteers does the center need?
   a. four
   b. five
   c. ten
   d. twenty

2. What can a volunteer do at this center?
   a. greet people
   b. help the art teachers
   c. serve food
   d. all of the above

3. How long do volunteers need to work?
   a. 1 hour a day
   b. 4 hours a day
   c. 8 hours a day
   d. 9 hours a day

4. Which statement is true?
   a. Volunteers must be artists.
   b. Volunteers must be experienced cooks.
   c. Volunteers must be over 21 years old.
   d. Volunteers must be team players.

B Talk with your classmates. Ask and answer the questions.

1. Have you ever volunteered in your community?
2. What did you do?

2 Fun with language

A Work with a partner. What volunteer work are the people doing?

Talk with your classmates. Discuss the questions.

1. What volunteer work is in your neighborhood or community?
2. What kind of volunteer work would you like to do?

B Play a game.

Sit in a circle.

One student says, "I borrowed some sugar, and I lent my car."

The next student says, "Iris borrowed some sugar, and she lent her car.
I borrowed a pen, and I lent my pencil."

Each student repeats and adds two more items.

The last student repeats everything.

3 Wrap up

Complete the **Self-assessment** on page 142.

Lesson A *Get ready*

1 Talk about the pictures

A What do you see?
B What is happening?
C What's the story?

2 Listening

A 💿 **Listen** and answer the questions.

1. Who are the speakers?
2. What are they talking about?

B 💿 **Listen again.** Put a check (✓) next to the doctor's advice.

1. ☐ sleep more   5. ☐ eat hamburgers
2. ✓ take a walk every day   6. ☐ eat fish
3. ☐ ride a bicycle   7. ☐ eat breakfast
4. ☐ take the elevator at work   8. ☐ take medication

Listen again. Check your answers.

C 💿 **Read.** Complete the story. Listen and check your answers.

advice	exercise	medication	tired
diet	health	pressure	weight

Stanley is at the doctor's office. His _____health_____ has always been
1
good, but he has been really _____ lately. The doctor looks
2
at Stanley's chart. He sees a couple of problems. One problem is
Stanley's _____ . He has gained 20 pounds. Another problem
3
is his blood _____ . The doctor tells him he needs regular
4
_____ – for example, walking or riding a bike. He also tells
5
Stanley to change his _____ – to eat more fish and vegetables.
6
If Stanley doesn't do these things, he will need to take pills and other
_____ . Stanley wants to be healthy, so he is going to try to
7
follow the doctor's _____ .
8

D **Talk** with a partner. Ask and answer the question.

What are three things you do to stay healthy?

Present perfect

1 Grammar focus: questions and statements with *recently* and *lately*

Questions

Have you gained weight recently?

Has Sheila gone to the gym lately?

Statements

I have gained weight recently.

Sheila hasn't gone to the gym lately.

Past participles

Regular verbs		Irregular verbs	
check → checked	start → started	eat → eaten	lose → lost
exercise → exercised	visit → visited	give → given	see → seen
gain → gained	weigh → weighed	go → gone	sleep → slept

For a complete grammar chart and explanation, turn to page 148.

For a list of irregular verbs, turn to page 151.

2 Practice

A Write. Complete the sentences. Use the present perfect.

Lola

Lola _____*has been*_____ unhappy recently.
1. be

She _____ to the gym lately. And she
2. not / go

_____ her weight. She _____
3. not / watch   4. not / eat

healthy food, either. She _____ a lot of
5. gain

weight, and her blood pressure _____ up, too.
6. go

William

William _____ to get in shape lately. He
7. start

_____ weight recently. His blood pressure
8. lose

_____ down, too. He _____
9. go   10. give up

hamburgers, French fries, and soft drinks. But he

_____ ice cream!
11. not / give up

Listen and check your answers.

B Talk with a partner. Ask and answer questions. Use the present perfect with *recently* and *lately*.

> **A** Has Elisa lost weight recently?
> **B** Yes, she has.

> **A** Has Roberto given up desserts lately?
> **B** No, he hasn't.

1

Elisa / lose weight

2

Roberto / give up desserts

3

Joy / start taking vitamins

4

Ahmet / gain weight

5

Martin and Julie / start exercising a lot

6

Lee / sleep much

Write a sentence about each picture. Use *recently* and *lately*.

Elisa has lost weight recently.

3 Communicate

A Work with a partner. Ask and answer questions. Complete the chart.

> **A** Have you eaten a lot of fish lately?
> **B** Yes, I have. How about you?

> **A** Have you had a cold lately?
> **B** No, I haven't. What about you?

Partner's name: _____	Yes	No
1. eat a lot of fish		
2. have a cold		
3. check your blood pressure		
4. see a doctor		
5. go to the gym		
6. visit a dentist		

B Share information about your partner.

Used to

1 Grammar focus: statements and questions

Statements	Yes / No questions	Short answers
I used to eat a lot of fatty foods. She used to go to bed late.	Did you use to exercise a lot? Did he use to eat a lot?	Yes, I did. No, he didn't.

For a complete grammar chart and explanation, turn to page 149.

2 Practice

A Write. Complete the sentences. Use *use to* or *used to*.

1. **A** Did he ____use to____ stay up all night?
   B Yes, he did, but he goes to bed early now.

2. **A** How often do you eat meat?
   B I _____ eat meat every night,
   but now I usually have fish.

3. **A** Did you _____ drive to work?
   B Yes, I did, but now I ride my bike.

4. **A** What do you usually do after work?
   B We _____ go straight home, but now we
   take dance classes twice a week.

5. **A** Do you exercise every day?
   B I _____ exercise every day, but now I
   exercise only on weekends.

🔊 **Listen** and check your answers. Then practice with a partner.

B **Work** with a partner. Talk about Michael as a young man and Michael today.

> Michael used to play sports, but now he watches sports on TV.

When Michael was young	Michael now
play sports	watch sports on TV
skip breakfast	eat three meals a day
take vitamins	not take vitamins
drink coffee	drink tea
sleep late	get up early
eat fruit between meals	eat sweets and chips between meals
work out every afternoon	take a nap every afternoon

Write sentences about Michael.

When Michael was young, he used to play sports. Now he watches sports on TV.

3 Communicate

A **Work** in a small group. Complete the sentences. Talk about your health habits.

1. When I was a child, I used to . . . , but now I . . .
2. In my country, I used to . . . , but now I . . .
3. When I was a teenager, I used to . . . , but now I . . .
4. When I first came to this country, I used to . . . , but now I . . .

B **Share** information about your classmates.

Lesson D Reading

1 Before you read

Look at the reading tip. Then read the first and last paragraphs.
Answer the questions.

1. Which plants is the reading about?
2. How long have people used them?

2 Read

SELF-STUDY
AUDIO CD

Read the magazine article. Listen and read again.

> The first paragraph of a reading is the introduction. It tells you the topic.
> The last paragraph is the conclusion. It often repeats the topic with different words.

Two Healthful Plants

Since the beginning of history, people in every culture have used plants to stay healthy and to prevent sickness. Garlic and chamomile are two healthful plants.

Garlic is a plant in the onion family. The green stem and the leaves of the garlic plant grow above the ground. The root – the part under the ground – is a bulb with sections called cloves. They look  like the pieces of an orange. The bulb is the part that people have traditionally used for medicine. They have used it for insect bites, cuts, earaches, and coughs. Today, some people also use it to treat high blood pressure and high cholesterol.

Chamomile is a small, pretty plant with flowers that bloom from late summer to early fall. The flowers have white petals and a yellow center. Many people use dried chamomile flowers to make tea.  Some people give the tea to babies with upset stomachs. They also drink chamomile tea to feel better when they have a cold or the flu, poor digestion, or trouble falling asleep.

For thousands of years, people everywhere have grown garlic, chamomile, and other herbal medicines in their gardens. Today, you can buy them in health-food stores. You can get them in dried, powdered, or pill form.

3 After you read

A Check your understanding.

1. What is the reading about?
2. What is the word for the sections of the garlic bulb?
3. How do people use garlic?
4. What does the chamomile plant look like?
5. What can you make from chamomile?
6. How do people use chamomile?
7. Which plant could you use for high blood pressure?

B Build your vocabulary.

1. Read the dictionary entry for *digestion*. What part of speech is it? What does it mean? What is the opposite word? What is the verb? What is the adjective?

> **digestion** /n/ the ability of the body to change food so the body can use it; *antonym* indigestion; /v/ digest; /adj/ digestive

2. Use a dictionary. Fill in the chart with the missing forms.

Noun	Verb	Adjective
digestion	digest	digestive
	prevent	
sickness		
	treat	
herbs		

3. Complete the sentences. Write the correct form of the word from Exercise B2.

a. You shouldn't swim right after you eat. You should wait to ____digest____ your food.

b. Chamomile, basil, oregano, and thyme are examples of _____ .

c. Some people can't drink milk. It makes them _____ .

d. Some people drink orange juice to _____ a cold or the flu. They don't want to get sick.

e. A hot bath is a good _____ for sore muscles.

C Talk with a partner. Ask and answer the questions.

1. How can you prevent a sore throat? a cold? weight gain?
2. What is the best treatment for a headache? a stomachache? an earache?
3. What herbs do you like to cook with? What's your favorite herb?

Lesson E Writing

1 Before you write

A **Work** in a small group. Look at the pictures. Match each plant with its use.

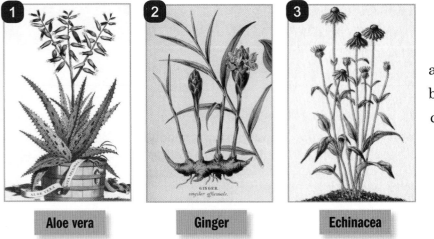

1 Aloe vera

2 Ginger

3 Echinacea

a. good for a cold _____
b. good for burns _____
c. good for a stomachache _____

B **Complete** the chart. Then add another healthful plant you know.

Plant	Description	Uses
Garlic	*bulb under the ground; green stem and leaves above the ground*	*insect bites, high blood pressure, cuts, earaches, cough, high cholesterol*
Chamomile		
Aloe vera		
Ginger		
Echinacea		

C Read the paragraph.

Licorice

Licorice is a popular herb in my native country, Greece. The plant has feathery leaves and purple flowers. It tastes sweet. My mother used to use licorice to make a medicine for my grandmother's arthritis. Mother grew the licorice plant in our backyard. She used to cut the licorice roots into pieces and put them inside a warm, wet cloth. Then she put the cloth on my grandmother's shoulder and knees. The licorice helped with the pain. Today, I use licorice when I have sore muscles.

Work with a partner. Put the information from the paragraph in order.

_____ how the writer's mother used the plant

_1_ where the plant grows

_____ how the plant helped

_____ how the plant tastes

_____ how the plant looks

_____ how the writer uses the plant today

> The first sentence of a paragraph is called the topic sentence. It names the topic and gives basic information about it.
>
> *Licorice* (topic) *is a popular herb in my native country, Greece* (basic information).

2 Write

Write a paragraph about a plant that people use as medicine. Use Exercises 1B and 1C to help you.

3 After you write

A Check your writing.

	Yes	No
1. In my topic sentence, I named the herb and gave basic information about it.	☐	☐
2. I described the plant.	☐	☐
3. I explained how people use the plant.	☐	☐

B Share your writing with a partner.

1. Take turns. Read your paragraph to a partner.
2. Comment on your partner's paragraph. Ask your partner a question about the paragraph. Tell your partner one thing you learned.

1 Life-skills reading

Medical History Form

1. Chief complaint: Describe the problem and approximately when it began.

Problem	Date problem began

2. Have you ever had any of the following?

☐ allergies	☐ back pain	☐ frequent headaches	☐ high blood pressure
☐ arthritis	☐ chest pains	☐ heart attack	☐ high cholesterol
☐ asthma	☐ diabetes	☐ heart disease	☐ tuberculosis

3. Are you pregnant?   Yes   No

4. Are you currently taking medications?   Yes   No

5. If yes, list all medications, including vitamins and herbal supplements.

_____

6. List any major illness, injury, or surgery that you have had in the past year.

_____

The above information is correct to the best of my knowledge.

7. Signature: _____   **8.** Date: _____

A **Read** the questions. Look at the form. Circle the answers.

1. Where do you write the reason for this doctor visit?
   a. number 1   c. number 4
   b. number 3   d. number 5

2. Where do you write the names of the medicines you take?
   a. number 2   c. number 5
   b. number 4   d. number 7

3. Where do you write that you had back surgery last year?
   a. number 1   c. number 5
   b. number 2   d. number 6

4. Where do you write when the problem began?
   a. number 1   c. number 5
   b. number 3   d. number 7

B **Work** with a partner. First, complete the form about yourself or someone you know. Then ask questions about your partner's form. Are the medical histories similar?

2 Fun with language

A **Talk** with your classmates. Complete the chart.

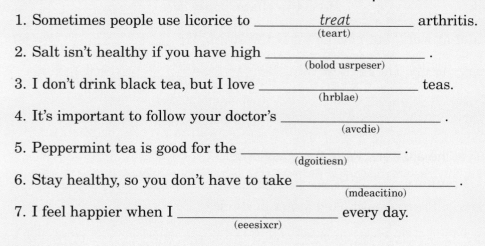

Ellen, did you use to eat desserts?

No, I didn't, but I do now.

Find someone who:	Name
didn't use to eat desserts	*Ellen*
used to exercise regularly	
used to be overweight	
has changed his or her diet recently	
always buys organic vegetables	
used to smoke	
has given up a food recently	
didn't use to eat a lot of fish	
has used herbal medicines	
rides a bicycle to school or work	

Share information about your classmates.

Ellen didn't use to eat desserts, but she eats them now.

B **Read** the sentences. Unscramble the words and complete the sentences.

1. Sometimes people use licorice to _____*treat*_____ arthritis.
   (teart)

2. Salt isn't healthy if you have high _____ .
   (bolod usrpeser)

3. I don't drink black tea, but I love _____ teas.
   (hrblae)

4. It's important to follow your doctor's _____ .
   (avcdie)

5. Peppermint tea is good for the _____ .
   (dgoitiesn)

6. Stay healthy, so you don't have to take _____ .
   (mdeacitino)

7. I feel happier when I _____ every day.
   (eeesixcr)

3 Wrap up

Complete the **Self-assessment** on page 142.

Review

1 Listening

Listen. Put a check (✓) under the correct name(s).

	Jenny	Sara
1. used to have time to call friends	✓	
2. used to work 50 hours a week		
3. used to exercise more		
4. used to cook healthy food		
5. used to take care of herself		
6. used to take the stairs at work		

Talk with a partner. Check your answers.

2 Grammar

A Write. Complete the story. Use the correct words.

A Happy Ending

Last year, Frank went to his doctor _____*because of*_____ his health. His doctor
         1. because / because of

told him that his blood pressure was _____ high. Frank got very
         2. enough / too

nervous because he didn't _____ have health problems.
         3. use to / used to

Frank _____ to get in shape lately. He _____ take
    4. started / has started   5. use to / used to

the elevator at work, but now he takes the stairs. He _____ a lot
         6. has / has had

more energy lately. The hardest thing he _____ recently is his
         7. has given up / gives up

favorite food – ice cream!

B Write. Look at the answers. Write the questions.

1. *A* _____ Frank _____ lately?

   B Yes, he has. Frank has started to get in shape.

2. *A* _____ Frank _____ ?

   B Yes. Frank went to the doctor last year because of his health.

3. *A* _____ Frank _____ ?

   B Yes, he did. Frank used to take the elevator at work.

Talk with a partner. Ask and answer the questions.

3 Pronunciation: voiced and voiceless *th* sounds

A 🔵 **Listen** to the *th* sounds in these phrases.

1. **th**is morning
2. sore **th**roat
3. **Th**at's too bad!
4. heal**th** problems

5. **th**e neighbors
6. on Sou**th** Street
7. **th**ey are
8. **th**is mon**th**

9. asked **th**em
10. **th**ree times
11. How are **th**ings?
12. **th**anks

🔵 **Listen again and repeat.**

B 🔵 **Listen and repeat.** Then underline the words with the *th* sounds.

1. **A** Where's Tommy this morning?
   B He's sick. He has a sore throat.
   A That's too bad!
   B He often has health problems.
   A I'm sorry to hear that.

2. **A** The neighbors on South Street are really noisy.
   B Yes, they are.
   A This month, I've asked them three times to be quiet.
   B Let's write them a letter.
   A That's a good idea.

Talk with a partner. Compare your answers.

C **Talk** with a partner. Practice the conversations. Pay attention to the words with the *th* sounds.

1. **A** What can your friends do to be more healthy?
   B Well, they can exercise more this month.
   A That's a good idea.
   B And they can eat healthy meals three times a day.

2. **A** How are things?
   B Not great. I have three tests this week.
   A Oh, I think you'll do fine.
   B Thanks.

D **Write** four questions. Use the words in Exercise 3A. Ask your partner.

Have you eaten this morning?

1. _____
2. _____
3. _____
4. _____

Lesson A Get ready

1 Talk about the pictures

A What do you see?
B What is happening?
C What's the story?

2 Listening

SELF-STUDY
AUDIO CD **A** **Listen** and answer the questions.

1. Who are the speakers?
2. What are they talking about?

SELF-STUDY
AUDIO CD **B** **Listen again.** Read and match the events. You may use an event more than once.

1. It opens at 10:00. __c__
2. It starts at 10:30. _____
3. It starts at 11:00. _____
4. The family will do this first. _____
5. The family will do this if the weather is nice. _____

a. outdoor concert
b. garden tour
c. art exhibit
d. storytelling

Listen again. Check your answers.

SELF-STUDY
AUDIO CD **C** **Read.** Complete the story. Listen and check your answers.

admission	concert	exhibit	storytelling
afford	events	options	tour

It is Thursday. Wen and Mei are talking about their plans for the weekend. They can't _____afford_____ to spend a lot of money on entertainment. They decide to check the newspaper for free community
1
_____ on Sunday. They have many _____ . There's
2   3
an outdoor _____ in the park, a walking _____ of
4   5
the gardens, a modern art _____ at the art museum, and
6
storytelling for children at the library. All these events have free

_____ .
7

The problem is that all these things are happening on Sunday at the same time. Mei and Wen decide to take their son to _____
8
first. Then, if the weather is nice, they will go to the concert. Later, they might go to the art museum.

D **Talk** with a partner. Ask and answer the question.

What kind of entertainment do you enjoy on the weekend?

Verbs + infinitives

1 Grammar focus: questions

Questions	Answers
Where do you plan to go?	I plan to go to the park.
Do you plan to go to the park?	Yes, I do. No, I don't.

Infinitives often follow these verbs:

agree	decide	hope	need	promise	want
(can / can't) afford	expect	intend	plan	refuse	would like

For a complete grammar chart and explanation, turn to page 147.
For a list of verbs that infinitives often follow, turn to page 147.

2 Practice

A Write. Complete the sentences.

1. **A** How much do you ___*expect to pay*___ for the concert?
   (expect / pay)

   B No more than $25.00.

2. **A** What have you _____ for your birthday?
   (decided / do)

   B I'm going to an exhibit at the art museum.

3. **A** Can you _____ a ticket for the show?
   (afford / buy)

   B Not really. I need to start saving money.

4. **A** What did you _____ next weekend?
   (agree / do)

   B We agreed to go to the park.

5. **A** How does Tom _____ to the park?
   (intend / get)

   B He's going to ride his bike.

6. **A** Have you ever _____ on a trip with your family?
   (refused / go)

   B No, I haven't.

7. **A** Did they _____ their relatives this weekend?
   (promise / visit)

   B Yes, they did.

> **Useful language**
> *afford to do something = have enough money to do it*

Listen and check your answers. Then practice with a partner.

B **Talk** with a partner. Ask and answer questions about Sharon's plans. Use the verbs in the box and an infinitive.

> **A** What does Sharon plan to do on Tuesday?
> **B** She plans to go to a concert with Linda.

expect	hope	intend	need	plan	want

May

Sunday	Monday	Tuesday	Wednesday	Thursday	Friday	Saturday
		1	2	3	4	5
		12:30 p.m. Go with Linda to a concert.	5:30 p.m. Meet Joe at the gym.	9:00 am. See the dentist.☹ 3:00 p.m. See the new art exhibit.	7:30 a.m. Go to work with John. 6:00 p.m. Have dinner with Andrew???	Sit on the beach all day!

Write sentences about Sharon's plans.

On Tuesday, Sharon plans to go to a concert with Linda.

3 Communicate

A **Work** in a small group. Choose one item from each column. Make sentences about your plans.

> I plan to meet my friends tomorrow.

expect		tomorrow
hope		next week
intend		next month
need	(infinitive of any verb)	next year
plan		two years from now
want		three years from now
would like		five years from now

B **Share** information about your classmates.

> Lidia plans to meet her friends tomorrow.

Present perfect

1 Grammar focus: *already* and *yet*

Questions

Have you bought the tickets yet?
Has she seen the movie already?

Short answers

| Yes, I have. | No, I haven't. |
| Yes, she has. | No, she hasn't. |

Affirmative statements

I've already bought the tickets.
She's already seen the movie.

Negative statements

I haven't bought the tickets yet.
She hasn't seen the movie yet.

Past participles
Irregular verbs

begin → begun	get → gotten	put → put
bring → brought	go → gone	read → read
buy → bought	make → made	set → set
do → done	pay → paid	

For a list of irregular verbs, turn to page 151.

2 Practice

A Write. Complete the sentences. Use *already* or *yet*.

1. It's 11:00 p.m. The salsa concert has ___already___ ended.

2. It's 8:00 a.m. The science museum opens at 9:00. It hasn't
   opened _____ .

3. It's July 5th. The Independence Day fair has _____ finished.

4. It's the beginning of August. School begins in September. School activities
   haven't begun _____ .

5. It's 2:00 a.m. The dance club stays open until 3:00. It hasn't
   closed _____ .

6. It's Friday evening. The weekend has _____ started.

7. It's 7:59 p.m. The movie starts at 8:00. We haven't missed
   the movie _____ .

8. It's Monday. I've _____ bought tickets for next Sunday's
   soccer game.

   Listen and check your answers.

B Talk with a partner. Jaime and Andrea are helping at their school's fund-raiser. Ask and answer questions about them. Use *yet*.

> **A** Has Jaime bought refreshments yet?
> **B** Yes, he has.
> **A** Has Andrea set up the tables yet?
> **B** No, she hasn't.

Culture note
A *fund-raiser* is an event where people collect money for a school, an organization, or a cultural activity.

Things to do before the fund-raiser

Jaime
- ✓ buy refreshments
- ✓ borrow more chairs
- call the chair-rental store
- get name tags
- pick up the DJ

Andrea
- set up the tables
- ✓ organize the volunteers
- ✓ make the food
- bring the music CDs
- ✓ put up the decorations

Write sentences about Jaime and Andrea. Use *already* and *yet*.

Jaime has already bought refreshments.
Andrea hasn't set up the tables yet.

3 Communicate

A Work with a partner. Ask and answer questions. Complete the chart.

> **A** Have you done your homework yet?
> **B** Yes, I have.
> **A** Have you paid your bills already?
> **B** No, I haven't.

Activities	Yes	No
1. do your homework		
2. pay your bills		
3. go to a baseball game in this country		
4. read the newspaper today		
5. (your question)		
6. (your question)		

B Share information about your classmates.

Lesson D *Reading*

1 Before you read

Talk with your classmates. Answer the questions.

1. Do you like salsa music?
2. Have you ever gone to an outdoor concert? Where? When?

2 Read

SELF-STUDY AUDIO CD

Read the concert review. Listen and read again.

> When you see a new word, try to guess if the meaning is positive or negative.
> *The volume was **excessive**.*
> *I had to wear my earplugs.*
> You can guess that *excessive* has a negative meaning.

SALSA STARZ
at Century Park

If you missed the outdoor concert at Century Park last Saturday evening, you missed a great night of salsa music and dancing – and the admission was free!

The performers were the popular band Salsa Starz. Bandleader Ernesto Sanchez led the five-piece group and two dancers. Sanchez is a versatile musician. He sang and played maracas and guitar. The other musicians were also superb. The group's excellent playing and great energy galvanized the crowd. No one sat down during the entire show!

However, the evening had some problems. At first, the sound level of the music was excessive. I had to wear earplugs. Then, the level was too low. The change in sound was irritating. In addition, the stage was plain and unremarkable. I expected to see lights and lots of color at the performance. The weather was another problem. The night started out clear. By 10:00 p.m., some ominous black clouds moved in, and soon it started to rain. The band intended to play until 11:00, but the show ended early because of the rain.

Century Park has free concerts every Saturday evening in July and August. If you haven't attended one of these concerts yet, plan to go next weekend. But take an umbrella!

3 After you read

A Check your understanding.

1. Where did the Salsa Starz perform?
2. What were two positive things about the concert?
3. What were three negative things?
4. Did the audience like the concert? How do you know?
5. How do you think the reviewer rated the performance? Find the words in the reading to support your opinion.

> **** excellent   *** very good   ** OK   * bad

B Build your vocabulary.

1. Find these words in the reading, and underline them. Which words are positive? Which words are negative? What clues helped you guess?

Word	Positive	Negative	Clue
1. versatile	✓		*He sang and played maracas and guitar.*
2. superb			
3. galvanized			
4. excessive			
5. irritating			
6. unremarkable			
7. ominous			

2. Work with your classmates. Write four more words in the reading that have a positive or negative meaning. Write P next to positive words. Write N next to negative words.

a. _____   c. _____

b. _____   d. _____

C Talk with a partner.

1. Tell about a superb restaurant.
2. Tell about a versatile artist.
3. Tell about an irritating experience.
4. Tell about an unremarkable TV program.

Lesson E *Writing*

1 Before you write

A Talk with your classmates.

1. Do you use e-mail? How often?
2. What do you use it for?

B Read the e-mail.

> To: Benito
> From: Renee
> Subject: Salsa concert
> Date: July 19, 2009
>
> Hi Benito,
>
> Thanks a million for telling me about the Salsa Starz show. It was FABULOUS! Ernesto Sanchez was incredible, and the music was awesome. Their energy was amazing! We danced for three hours!! Small problem: We got there late, so we had to stand in the back. It was hard to see. BIG problem: the weather! Early in the evening, it was clear. Then around 10:00, it started to rain. And it was C-O-L-D! ☹ Next time, I plan to take a sweater and an umbrella. Next time, I hope you can come, too.
>
> Miss you!
> Renee

Work with a partner. Complete the diagram with positive and negative information about the concert.

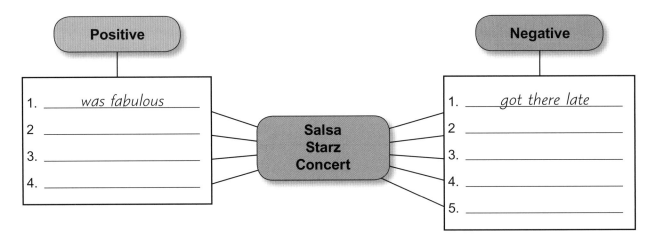

Positive
1. _was fabulous_
2. _____
3. _____
4. _____

Salsa Starz Concert

Negative
1. _got there late_
2. _____
3. _____
4. _____
5. _____

C **Write** the name of a concert, a movie, or a performance you have seen in the middle of the diagram. Complete the diagram with positive and negative information.

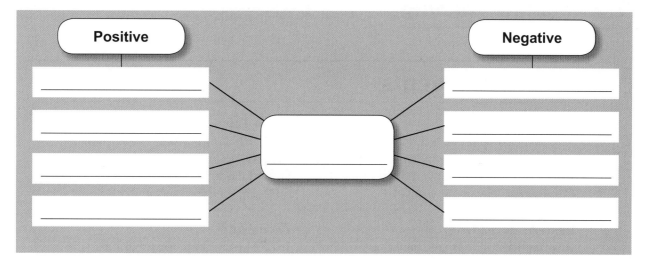

Positive		Negative
_____		_____
_____	_____	_____
_____		_____
_____		_____

Share your information with a partner.

2 Write

Write an e-mail about a concert, a movie, or a performance you have seen. Use Exercises 1B and 1C to help you.

The style of a friendly e-mail is informal.
- Some sentences are not complete.
  Miss you!
  BIG problem: the weather!
- Writers use capital letters and symbols to express their feelings.
  It was FABULOUS!
  It was C-O-L-D! ☹

3 After you write

A **Check** your writing.

	Yes	No
1. I named the event in my first sentence.	☐	☐
2. I used positive and negative words to describe the event.	☐	☐
3. I used an informal writing style in my e-mail.	☐	☐

B **Share** your writing with a partner.

1. Take turns. Read your e-mail to a partner.
2. Comment on your partner's e-mail. Ask your partner a question about the e-mail. Tell your partner one thing you learned.

1 Life-skills reading

Announcements

Travel Movies
Join us at 7:00 p.m. on Saturday and Sunday to see movies on India, Japan, and Brazil. Kids welcome. Downtown Public Library. Come early – seating is limited.

Concerts on the Green
Hear the Riverside Brass Band every Friday this month at noon. North end of City Park, near the courthouse.

Crafts Fair
Find gifts for your family and friends. Jewelry, pottery, paintings, and food from around the world. Sunday from 9:00 a.m. to 5:00 p.m. at Broadway and 5th Street.

Fix a Flat
Bike Master Shop offers basic bicycle maintenance clinics this Saturday at 4:30 p.m. and Sunday at 9:00 a.m. in front of the Bike Master Shop.

A **Read** the questions. Look at the announcements. Circle the answers.

1. At which event can you buy food?
   a. Concerts on the Green
   b. Crafts Fair
   c. Travel Movies
   d. all of the above

2. Which event does not happen during the day?
   a. Concerts on the Green
   b. Crafts Fair
   c. Fix a Flat
   d. Travel Movies

3. Which event would be good for bike riders?
   a. Crafts Fair
   b. Fix a Flat
   c. Travel Movies
   d. none of the above

4. Which event is at noon on Saturday?
   a. Concerts on the Green
   b. Fix a Flat
   c. Travel Movies
   d. none of the above

B **Talk** with a partner. Ask and answer the questions.

1. Which activity would you like to attend? Why?
2. What other activities or events do you like to attend?

2 Fun with language

A Write the activities.

| bike riding | eating | listening to music | people watching | walking |

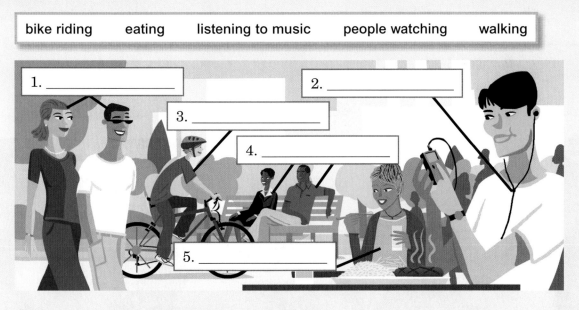

1. _____

2. _____

3. _____

4. _____

5. _____

B Talk with your classmates. Complete the chart.

> **A** What is your favorite place around town to walk?
> **B** Stanley Park.
> **C** Golden Green Park.

What is your favorite place around town . . .	Your group's ideas
to walk?	*Stanley Park, Golden Green Park*
to watch people?	
to ride a bicycle?	
to see a movie?	
to have lunch?	
to listen to music?	
to dance?	
to go with your family?	
to shop?	

Share information with your classmates. Vote on the best places.

3 Wrap up

Complete the **Self-assessment** on page 143.

Get ready

1 Talk about the pictures

A What do you see?
B What is happening?
C What's the story?

Time

2 Listening

A 🔊 **Listen** and answer the questions.

1. Who are the speakers?
2. What are they talking about?

B 🔊 **Listen again.** Complete Winston's to-do list.

> **Things to Do**
> 1. trash
> 2.
> 3.
> 4.
> 5.

Listen again. Check your answers.

C 🔊 **Read.** Complete the story. Listen and check your answers.

chores	due	prioritize	tasks
deadline	impatient	procrastinating	

Winston is listening to music in his room. His mother comes in and tells him to stop ___procrastinating___ . She is very _____ because he
1   2
isn't taking out the trash and he isn't doing his homework.

Winston has too many things to do. His mother suggests making a to-do list. First, she tells him to list all the tasks he needs to do. Next, she tells him to _____ – to put his _____ in order of importance.
3   4
Winston wants to practice guitar first because it's the most fun. His mother says he needs to do his homework and _____ first. He decides to
5
do his English and math homework first because they are _____
6
the next day. He also has a history project, but the _____ is next
7
Tuesday. After he finishes his homework, he will practice guitar. But before he does anything else, he has to take out the trash.

D **Talk** with a partner. Ask and answer the question.

When you have a lot of things to do, how do you decide what to do first?

Dependent clauses

1 Grammar focus: clauses with *when*

When I have a lot to do, I make a to-do list.
When she feels tired, she takes a break.

I make a to-do list when I have a lot to do.
She takes a break when she feels tired.

For a grammar explanation, turn to page 153.

Useful language
Use a comma after *when* clauses at the beginning of a sentence. When you read out loud, pause after the comma.

2 Practice

A Write. Combine the sentences. Use *when*.

Tips for Managing Your Time

1. You have many things to do. Make a to-do list.
   When *you have many things to do* , *make a to-do list* .
2. You have a deadline. Write it on your calendar.
   When _____ , _____ .
3. Don't let people interrupt you. You need to concentrate.
   _____ when _____ .
4. You want to focus on a task. Turn off the television.
   When _____ , _____ .
5. You feel tired. Take a break.
   When _____ , _____ .
6. Give yourself a reward. You finish something difficult.
   _____ when _____ .
7. Don't procrastinate. You have a deadline.
   _____ when _____ .
8. You are tired. Don't do difficult tasks.
   When _____ , _____ .

Listen and check your answers.

B **Talk** with a partner. Make sentences with *when*.

> **A** When Mr. Jackson has a deadline, he doesn't answer the phone.
> **B** Ms. Clark answers every call when she has a deadline.

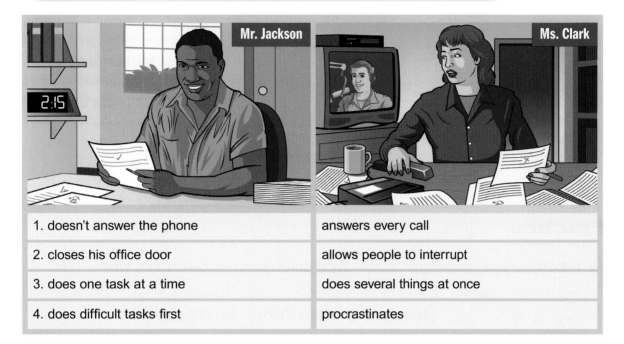

Mr. Jackson	Ms. Clark
1. doesn't answer the phone	answers every call
2. closes his office door	allows people to interrupt
3. does one task at a time	does several things at once
4. does difficult tasks first	procrastinates

Write sentences about Mr. Jackson and Ms. Clark.

Mr. Jackson doesn't answer the phone when he has a deadline.

3 Communicate

A **Work** in a small group. Interview your classmates. Complete the chart.

> **A** What do you do when you have a deadline?
> **B** I usually procrastinate.
> **C** I start working right away.

What do you do when you . . .	Name: _____	Name: _____
have a deadline?		
have many things to do?		
finish a difficult task?		
have trouble concentrating?		
(your idea)		

B **Share** information about your classmates.

Lesson C *Dependent clauses*

1 Grammar focus: clauses with *before* and *after*

Before she eats breakfast, she reads the newspaper.
After I watch the news, I eat dinner.

She reads the newspaper before she eats breakfast.
I eat dinner after I watch the news.

For a grammar explanation, turn to page 153.

Useful language
Use a comma when *after* and *before* clauses are at the beginning of a sentence.

2 Practice

A Read Bonnie's morning schedule. Write sentences with *before* and *after*.

Bonnie's morning schedule

6:55 take a shower
7:15 get dressed
7:30 make coffee

7:35 bring in the newspaper
7:40 eat breakfast
8:00 leave for work

take a shower / get dressed

1. After *Bonnie takes a shower* , *she gets dressed* .
2. *Bonnie takes a shower* before *she gets dressed* .

get dressed / make coffee

3. Before _____ , _____ .
4. _____ after _____ .

bring in the newspaper / eat breakfast

5. _____ before _____ .
6. _____ after _____ .

eat breakfast / leave for work

7. After _____ , _____ .
8. Before _____ , _____ .

Listen and check your answers.

B Talk with a partner. Talk about Chul, a soap-opera star. Use *before* and *after*.

> *A* Before Chul goes to the studio, he works out.
> *B* After Chul works out, he goes to the studio.

works out

goes to the studio

memorizes his lines

puts on makeup

performs his scene

goes home and rests

Write sentences about Chul's day.

Chul works out before he goes to the studio.

3 Communicate

A Work in a small group. Ask and answer questions about daily activities. Complete the chart.

> *A* What do you do every day, Emma?
> *B* I study.
> *A* What do you do before you study?
> *B* I watch TV.

> *A* What do you do after you study?
> *B* I go to bed.

Name	Activity	Before activity	After activity
Emma	study	watch TV	go to bed

B Share information about your classmates.

Lesson D Reading

1 Before you read

Look at the title. Answer the questions.

1. What are some rules about time in this country?
2. What are some rules about time in other countries?

2 Read

SELF-STUDY
AUDIO CD

Read this article. Listen and read again.

RULES ABOUT TIME

Every culture has rules about time. These rules are usually unspoken, but everybody knows them.

In some countries such as the United States, England, and Canada, punctuality is an unspoken rule. It is important to be on time, especially in business. People usually arrive a little early for business appointments. Business meetings often have strict beginning and ending times. When you are late, other people might think you are rude, disorganized, or irresponsible.

These countries also have cultural rules about time in social situations. For example, when an invitation for dinner says 6:00 p.m., it is impolite to arrive more than five or ten minutes late. On the other hand, when the invitation is for a cocktail party from 6:00 to 8:00 or a reception from 3:30 to 5:30, you can arrive anytime between those hours. For public events with specific starting times – movies, concerts, plays – you should arrive a few minutes before the event begins. In fact, some theaters do not allow people to enter if they arrive after the event has started.

Other cultures have different rules about time. In Brazil, it is not unusual for guests to arrive an hour or two after a social event begins. In the Philippines, it is not uncommon for people to miss scheduled events – a class or an appointment – to meet a friend at the airport. Many Filipinos believe that relationships with people are more important than keeping a schedule.

> Dashes often signal a definition, explanation, or example. The dashes in this reading signal examples.

76   Unit 6

3 After you read

A Check your understanding.

1. What are "unspoken" rules?
2. What is the author's definition of "on time"? What is your definition of "on time"?
3. What are examples of public events with specific starting times?
4. When should you arrive for the following events in the U.S.? When should you arrive for these same events in your native country?
   - a medical appointment
   - a business meeting
   - dinner at someone's house
   - a party
   - a sports event

B Build your vocabulary.

1. English has several prefixes that mean "not." Write words from the reading that begin with these prefixes.

un- _unspoken_

dis- _____

ir- _____

im- _____

2. Work with a partner. Explain the meaning of the words you wrote.

3. Work with a partner. Write more words with the prefixes. Use each word in a sentence.

un-	dis-	ir-	im-

C Talk with a partner. Ask and answer the questions.

1. Your friend is disorganized. What advice can you give your friend?
2. Someone is late to a job interview. Is that person irresponsible? Why or why not?
3. You are 30 minutes late for lunch with a friend. Is it impolite? Why or why not?

1 Before you write

A Work in a small group. Discuss the questions. Complete the diagrams.

1. What qualities and habits does a good time manager have?

_____ *makes a to-do list* _____

Good time manager

_____

_____

_____

_____

2. What qualities and habits does a weak time manager have?

_____ *procrastinates* _____

Weak time manager

_____

_____

_____

_____

B Talk with a partner. Answer the questions.

1. What qualities and habits from each diagram do you have?
2. In general, are you a good time manager or a weak time manager? Why do you think so?

C Read the paragraph.

A Weak Time Manager

Lucinda is not a very good time manager. For example, this is the way she does her homework. First, she sits down and takes out her books. Two minutes later, she decides to get a cup of coffee. She goes to the kitchen, makes coffee, and returns to her desk. Before she starts reading, she checks her e-mail. Then the phone rings. It's her best friend. They talk for 20 minutes. After they hang up, it's 9:00 p.m. – time for Lucinda's favorite TV show. She watches the show from 9:00 to 10:00. Then, she studies from 10:00 until 1:30 a.m. Of course, she is tired in the morning. In summary, Lucinda is a weak time manager because she procrastinates.

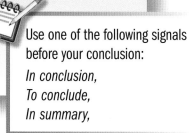

Use one of the following signals before your conclusion:

In conclusion,

To conclude,

In summary,

Work with a partner. Answer the questions.

1. What is the topic sentence?
2. How many examples does the writer give about Lucinda?
3. Which words signal the conclusion?

2 Write

Write a paragraph about someone you know who is a good or a weak time manager. Use Exercises 1A and 1C to help you.

3 After you write

A Check your writing.

	Yes	No
1. My topic sentence says what kind of time manager I am writing about.	☐	☐
2. I included examples to support my topic sentence.	☐	☐
3. I used a signal before my conclusion.	☐	☐

B Share your writing with a partner.

1. Take turns. Read your paragraph to a partner.
2. Comment on your partner's paragraph. Ask your partner a question about the paragraph. Tell your partner one thing you learned.

Another view

1 Life-skills reading

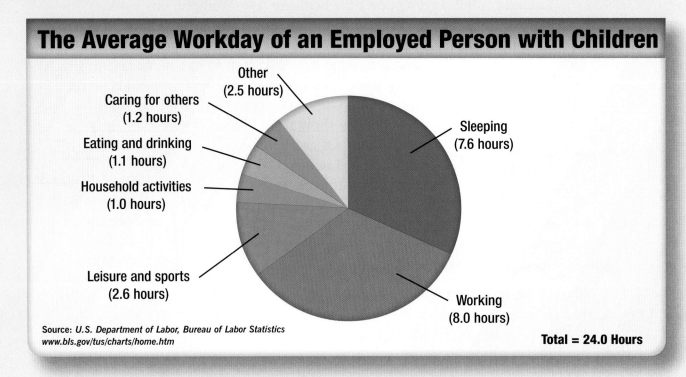

The Average Workday of an Employed Person with Children

Other
(2.5 hours)

Caring for others
(1.2 hours)

Eating and drinking
(1.1 hours)

Household activities
(1.0 hours)

Leisure and sports
(2.6 hours)

Sleeping
(7.6 hours)

Working
(8.0 hours)

Source: *U.S. Department of Labor, Bureau of Labor Statistics*
www.bls.gov/tus/charts/home.htm

Total = 24.0 Hours

A Read the questions. Look at the pie chart. Circle the answers.

1. Who is this chart about?
   a. employed people with children
   b. employed people without children
   c. unemployed people with children
   d. none of the above

2. Which activity do these people spend the least time doing?
   a. caring for others
   b. eating and drinking
   c. household activities
   d. none of the above

3. Which activity do these people spend the most time doing?
   a. eating and drinking
   b. leisure and sports
   c. working
   d. none of the above

4. Which statement is true?
   a. People spend more time eating, drinking, and sleeping than working.
   b. People spend more time working than eating, drinking, and sleeping.
   c. People spend as much time eating, drinking, and sleeping as working.
   d. none of the above

B Talk with a partner. Ask and answer the questions.

1. About how much time a day do you spend on the activities listed on the pie chart?
2. On which activities do you spend more time than the chart shows?
3. On which activities do you spend less time than the chart shows?

2 Fun with language

A **Work** in a small group. Look at the pictures. Read the idioms.
What does each idiom mean?

When traffic is slow, we **save time** by taking the train.

Take your time when you do dangerous work.

Celia didn't leave her house **in time** to catch her bus.

On weekends, Harry loves to **spend time** relaxing and reading.

Rose always arrives **on time** for her appointments.

My son has to stop **wasting time** and do his homework.

B **Talk** with a partner. Ask and answer the questions.

1. What can you do to save time?
2. Do you usually leave your home in time for class, or are you often late?
3. How do you like to spend your free time?
4. Do you ever waste time? How?

3 Wrap up

Complete the **Self-assessment** on page 143.

Review

1 Listening

Listen. Put a check (✓) under the correct name.

	Trina	Minh
1. has decided to visit his family		✓
2. is going to Las Vegas		
3. hasn't bought plane tickets yet		
4. has already made reservations		
5. won a free hotel room		

Talk with a partner. Check your answers.

2 Grammar

A Write. Complete the story. Use the correct words.

A Great Time Manager

Natalia Alvarez begins work at 8:00 in the morning. It is 7:50 and she has

already _____*arrived*_____ at her job. She is a single parent, so she needs
      1. arrive / arrived

_____ her time well. Every Saturday _____ she goes
2. manage / to manage   3. before / after

shopping, she makes a list of all the food she needs. _____ she takes
                                               4. When / After

her children to the park on Sunday, she cooks meals for the rest of the week.

When she _____ home late, she just heats up the food she cooked on
         5. has come / comes

Sunday. After she helps her children with homework, she _____ the
                                                         6. do / does

laundry and goes to bed. Natalia is a great time manager.

B Write. Look at the answers. Write the questions.

1. **A** What does Natalia do before _____ ?

   B Natalia makes a list before she goes shopping.

2. **A** What _____ ?

   B She cooks meals for the rest of the week after she goes to the park.

3. **A** When _____ ?

   B She does the laundry after she helps her children with homework.

Talk with a partner. Ask and answer the questions.

3 Pronunciation: initial *st* sound

A 💿 **Listen** to the initial *st* sound.

1. **St**udy English.
2. **St**art the computer.
3. Tell the **st**ory.
4. What **st**ate do you live in?
5. Go to the **st**ore.
6. **St**udents need to **st**udy.
7. Let's see the Salsa **St**arz.
8. **St**op procrastinating.

💿 **Listen again and repeat.**

B 💿 **Listen and repeat.** Then underline the initial *st* sound.

1. *A* Hi, Stuart. I'm going to the store. What do you need?

   B Can you get me some stamps? It's the first of the month, and I have to pay bills.

   A Sure.

   B Thanks. I'll start writing the checks now and stop procrastinating.

2. *A* Hello, Stephanie.

   B Hi, Steve. Are you still a student here?

   A Yes. I'm studying appliance repair.

   B Really? Maybe you can fix my stove when you're finished.

   A I hope so.

Talk with a partner. Compare your answers.

C **Talk** with a partner. Ask and answer the questions. Say the words with the initial *st* sound carefully.

1. How long have you studied at this school?
2. When you go to the store, what do you usually buy?
3. When did you move to this state?
4. When did you start working?

D **Write** five questions. Use the following words. Ask your partner the questions. Remember to pay attention to the initial *st* sound.

1. study: _____

2. store: _____

3. start: _____

4. story: _____

5. student: _____

Get ready

1 Talk about the pictures

A What do you see?
B What is happening?
C What's the story?

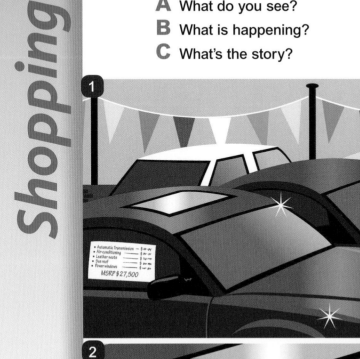

Big Summer Savings

Julie   Ken

- Automatic Transmission — $ w·ʊ
- Air-conditioning ——— $ w·ʊ
- Leather seats ——— $ 1u·ʊ
- Sun roof ——— $ w·ʊ
- Power windows ——— $ w·ʊ
  MSRP $ 27,500

- Automatic Transmission — $ w·ʊ
- Air-conditioning ——— $ w·ʊ
- Leather seats ——— $ 1u·ʊ
- Sun roof ——— $ w·ʊ
- Power windows ——— $ w·ʊ

MSRP $ 27,500

Ask About Low-Interest Financing

BOB'S USED CARS AND TRUCKS

BOB'S USED CARS AND TRUCKS

2 Listening

A 🎵 **Listen** and answer the questions.

1. Who are the speakers?
2. What are they talking about?

B 🎵 **Listen again.** Complete the chart.

	How much / many?
1. cost of a new car	$27,500
2. cost of a car with tax and fees	
3. money in the savings account	
4. interest rate (%)	
5. months to pay	
6. cost of a used car	

Listen again. Check your answers.

C 🎵 **Read.** Complete the story. Listen and check your answers.

afford	balance	cash	credit	debt	financing	interest	pay off

Ken and his wife, Julie, are looking at cars. Ken wants to buy a new car

that costs over $27,000. Julie thinks that they can't ____afford____ to spend
                                                              1

that much money. The _____ in their savings account is less than
                          2

$8,000. She's afraid of getting into _____ . But Ken says they can get
                                          3

_____ to help pay for the new car. The _____ rate is low, and
      4   5

they can take five years to _____ the loan. Ken isn't worried about
                                  6

buying things on _____ .
                        7

Julie disagrees. She suggests that they could buy a used car. She says her

father never had a credit card. He always

paid _____ for everything.
          8

Useful language

*To buy on credit means to buy something
now and pay for it later.*

D **Talk** with a partner. Ask and answer the questions.

1. What things do people often buy on credit?
2. Is it a good idea to buy things on credit? Why or why not?

1 Grammar focus: *could* and *should*

could for suggestions

You could get a smaller car and save money.
He could keep his money in a savings account.

should for advice

What should I do?   You should open a savings account.

For a complete grammar chart, turn to page 150.

2 Practice

A Write. Complete the sentences. Use *could* or *should*.

1. **A** My rent is going up again. What should I do?

   B Here's my advice. You're a good tenant. I think you ____should____ talk to your landlord.

2. **A** I have to fix my credit. What should I do?

   B You _____ talk to a debt counselor. He can help you.

3. **A** Can you suggest a nice restaurant? It's my wife's birthday.

   B You _____ try Chao's. Or how about Anita's?

4. **A** It's my niece's 16th birthday next week. What could I get her?

   B Why don't you get tickets to a concert? Or you _____ buy her a CD.

5. **A** That vocational school is very expensive. I can't afford it. Can you give me any advice?

   B Well, you're a good student. I think you _____ apply for a scholarship.

6. **A** I need a new car. Where do you suggest I look for one?

   B How about looking in the newspaper? Or

   you _____ look online.

   🔊 **Listen** and check your answers. Then practice with a partner.

Useful language

For suggestions, you can say:

Why don't you + verb . . . ?
How about + noun . . . ?
How about + verb + -ing . . . ?

B **Talk** with a partner. Take turns. Read the problems. Make suggestions or give advice.

> **A** My car broke down. I need to go to work.
> **B** You could take the bus, or you could ask someone for a ride.

"My car broke down. I need to go to work."

"My rent is going up $150!"

"It's getting cold in here."

"I can't afford a new washing machine."

"These shoes look terrible."

"I don't have enough cash to pay for these groceries."

Write a suggestion or advice for each picture.

You could take the bus, or you could ask someone for a ride.

3 Communicate

A **Work** in a small group. Make suggestions or give advice.

- Helene spends too much money on food.
- Gregory spends too much money on clothes.
- Teresa spends too much money on rent.
- Youssef spends too much money on cell phone calls.

B **Share** your ideas with your classmates.

Lesson C · *Gerunds*

1 Grammar focus: gerunds after prepositions

I'm thinking about buying a car.
She's afraid of losing her job.
They're interested in applying for a loan.

Gerunds often follow these phrases:

afraid of	thank (someone) for
excited about	think about
happy about	tired of
interested in	worried about

For a complete grammar chart and explanation, turn to page 146.
For a list of phrases that gerunds often follow, turn to page 146.

2 Practice

A Write. Complete the sentences. Use gerunds.

1. I'm worried about _____*paying*_____ interest on my credit card balance.
   (pay)

2. Rob is afraid of _____ into debt. He pays for everything with cash.
   (get)

3. Have you thought about _____ a checking account?
   (open)

4. Elizabeth is happy about _____ an apartment she can afford.
   (find)

5. Elena is excited about _____ classes at the community college.
   (start)

6. I'm tired of _____ payments on my car.
   (make)

7. Franco isn't interested in _____ for a loan.
   (apply)

8. Thank you for _____ me money for school.
   (lend)

9. We're thinking about _____ a house.
   (buy)

10. They were worried about _____ a loan.
    (get)

🔘 **Listen** and check your answers.

88   Unit 7

B **Talk** with a partner. Ask and answer questions.

> **A** What's she happy about?
> **B** She's happy about opening a checking account.

happy about /
open a checking account

thinking about /
buy a computer

worried about /
be in debt

interested in /
study auto mechanics

tired of /
wait in line

excited about /
buy a new car

Write a sentence about each picture.

She's happy about opening a checking account.

3 Communicate

A **Work** in a small group. Ask and answer questions.

afraid of	happy about	think about
excited about	interested in	tired of

> **A** What are you thinking about?
> **B** I'm thinking about paying my rent.

B **Share** information about your classmates.

1 Before you read

Look at the reading tip. Skim the magazine article. Answer the questions.

1. What problem did the people have?
2. How did they solve it?

2 Read

SELF-STUDY
AUDIO CD **Read** the magazine article. Listen and read again.

A Credit Card Nightmare

One way to organize information is to give problems and solutions.

Sun Hi and Joseph Kim got their first credit card a week after they got married. At first, they paid off the balance every month.

The couple's problems began after they bought a new house. They bought new furniture, a big-screen television, and two new computers. To pay for everything, they applied for more and more credit. Soon they had six different credit cards, and they were more than $18,000 in debt.

"It was a nightmare!" says Mrs. Kim. "The interest rates were 19 percent to 24 percent. Our minimum payments were over $750 a month. We both got second jobs, but it wasn't enough. I was so worried about paying off the debt, I cried all the time."

Luckily, the Kims found a solution. They met Dolores Delgado, a debt counselor. With her help, they looked at all of their living expenses and made a family budget. They combined their six credit card payments into one monthly payment with a lower interest rate. Now, their monthly budget for all living expenses is $3,400. Together they earn $3,900 a month. That leaves $500 for paying off their debt.

"We've cut up our credit cards," says Mr. Kim. "No more expensive furniture! In five years, we can pay off our debt. Now we know. Credit cards are dangerous!"

3 After you read

A Check your understanding.

1. When did Mr. and Mrs. Kim get their first credit card?
2. When did their problems begin?
3. How did they pay for everything?
4. Mrs. Kim says, "It was a nightmare!" What does she mean?
5. Who is Dolores Delgado, and how did she help them?
6. Do you think the Kims will have financial problems in the future? Why or why not?

B Build your vocabulary.

1. Find these words in the reading, and underline them.

credit card   interest rates   minimum payments   debt counselor   family budget

2. Work with a partner. Circle the correct answers.

1. Look at the words in Exercise B1. In each of the two-word combinations, the first word is:
   a. a noun   b. an adjective
2. Look at the words again. The second word is:
   a. a noun   b. an adjective

3. Match each phrase with its meaning.

1. credit card _____
2. interest rate _____
3. minimum payment _____
4. debt counselor _____
5. family budget _____

   a. a spending plan that a family makes for itself
   b. a small plastic card that allows you to buy something now and pay for it later
   c. the smallest payment you can make each month on a credit card
   d. the rate – percentage – of interest that you must pay each month on a credit card
   e. a person who helps you solve financial problems

4. Work with your classmates. Write other *noun + noun* combinations.

_____   _____   _____

C Talk with your classmates. Ask and answer the questions.

1. How many credit cards do you have? What interest rate do you pay?
2. Do you pay the minimum payment each month?
3. Do you think a family budget is important? Why or why not?

Lesson E *Writing*

1 Before you write

A **Talk** with a partner. Look at the picture. What is the problem?
What do you suggest?

B **Read** the letter from a newspaper advice column.

The Money Man

Dear Money Man,

    I recently got a new job in a downtown office. I need to look nice every day. I've never worked in an office before, and I don't have the right clothes. Most of the women wear suits to work. How can I get a new wardrobe without spending my entire salary? Can you give me advice?

Not Clothes Crazy

Work with a partner. Answer the questions.

1. What is the woman's problem?
2. What do you suggest?

C **Read** the answer from the Money Man.

Dear Not Clothes Crazy,

It's important to look nice on your job, but you don't need to spend all your money on clothes. I have a few suggestions. First, why don't you buy a black suit with a skirt, jacket, and pants? Then wear a different blouse and jewelry every day for a different look. Second, you could shop at thrift stores. They often have excellent used clothes at very cheap prices. Third, how about talking to the other women in your office? They can tell you about good places to shop. Finally, you should make a monthly budget and follow it carefully. That is the most important thing.

Money Man

> Use words like *first, second, third,* and *finally* to list your ideas.

Work with a partner. What does the Money Man suggest?

2 Write

Read the letter. Write an answer. Use Exercises 1A, 1B, and 1C to help you.

Dear Money Man,

My wife and I have three young children. We both work full-time. When we come home from work, we are very tired and don't want to cook. We eat in fast-food restaurants three or four times a week. It's very expensive. Last night, the bill was $44! How can we save money on dinner?

Fast-Food Dad

3 After you write

A **Check** your writing.

	Yes	No
1. I started with the problem.	☐	☐
2. I wrote two or more suggestions.	☐	☐
3. I used words like *first* and *second* to list my suggestions.	☐	☐

B **Share** your writing with a partner.

1. Take turns. Read your letter to a partner.
2. Comment on your partner's letter. Ask your partner a question about the letter. Tell your partner one thing you learned.

Another view

1 Life-skills reading

<u>TOWN ▲ BANK</u>   **Checking Accounts**

Choose the plan that's right for you!

	Regular Checking	Premium Checking
Monthly Service Fee	$8	$12
Minimum Daily Balance (to waive the monthly service fee)	$1,000	$5,000
Earn Interest	No	Yes
ATM and Bank Card	Free	Free
Free Checks	No	Yes
Free Internet Banking	Yes	Yes
Free Internet Bill Paying	No	Yes
Free Money Orders and Traveler's Checks	No	Yes

A Read the questions. Look at the bank brochure. Circle the answers.

1. What does the Regular Checking plan offer?
   a. a free bank card
   b. free checks
   c. free money orders
   d. none of the above

2. What does the Premium Checking plan offer?
   a. a free ATM card
   b. a free bank card
   c. free traveler's checks
   d. all of the above

3. With Premium Checking, how much do you need in your account to avoid a monthly service fee?
   a. 0
   b. $12
   c. $1,000
   d. $5,000

4. Which kind of checking offers free Internet banking?
   a. Premium Checking
   b. Regular Checking
   c. both *a* and *b*
   d. neither *a* nor *b*

B Talk with your classmates. Ask and answer the questions.

1. Do you have a checking account? Do you pay a monthly fee? What services does your bank offer you?
2. Which of the accounts from Town Bank would be better for you? Why?

2 Fun with language

A Talk with your classmates. Ask and answer questions. Complete the chart.

> *A* Juan, do you like paying cash for everything?
> *B* Yes, I do.

Find a classmate who:	Name
1. likes paying cash for everything	*Juan*
2. enjoys buying presents for friends	
3. likes to shop at garage sales and thrift stores	
4. eats in a restaurant twice a week	
5. has more than one credit card	
6. likes to save money	
7. enjoys spending money on jewelry	
8. usually sends money to family members	

Share information about your classmates.

B Play a game.

Sit in a circle.
Say a sentence about yourself.
Use a phrase from the box and a gerund.
Your classmate repeats your sentence and adds his or her sentence.
Continue around the circle.

afraid of	think about
excited about	tired of
happy about	worried about
interested in	

> *A* I'm excited about visiting my family in Egypt.
> *B* Ahmed is excited about visiting his family in Egypt. I'm tired of cleaning the house.
> *C* Ahmed is excited about visiting his family in Egypt. Shira is tired of cleaning her house. I'm thinking about buying a new car.

3 Wrap up

Complete the **Self-assessment** on page 144.

Lesson A *Get ready*

1 Talk about the pictures

A What do you see?
B What is happening?
C What's the story?

Tony

RESUME

Human Resources

RESUME

Mr. Leong

2 Listening

SELF-STUDY
AUDIO CD

A **Listen** and answer the questions.

1. Who are the speakers?
2. What are they talking about?

SELF-STUDY
AUDIO CD

B **Listen again.** Complete the chart with information about Tony.

Topic	Tony's answers
1. job he is applying for	*shipping-and-receiving clerk*
2. native country	
3. current job	
4. office machines he can use	
5. strengths	
6. shift he prefers	

Listen again. Check your answers.

SELF-STUDY
AUDIO CD

C **Read.** Complete the story. Listen and check your answers.

background	employed	personnel	shift
degree	gets along	reliable	strengths

Tony has been working as a teacher's assistant for about a year. He is also going to college part-time to get a ___degree___ in accounting. Right now, Tony
1
is at a job interview with Mr. Leong, the _____ manager.
2

Mr. Leong asks about Tony's _____ . Tony says he is from Peru and
3
has been living in the United States for two years. Next, Mr. Leong asks about Tony's work experience, and Tony says that now he is _____ at an
4
elementary school. Finally, Mr. Leong asks about Tony's personal _____ .
5
Tony says he is responsible and _____ , and he _____ with
6   7
everybody. Tony says he prefers to work the day _____ . Mr. Leong says
8
he will contact Tony next week.

D **Talk** with a partner. Ask and answer the questions.

Have you ever had a job interview? What happened?

Present perfect continuous

1 Grammar focus: questions and statements

Questions

Have you been living here for a long time?
Has Tony been working here for a long time?

How long have you been looking for a job?
How long has Tony been working as a teacher's assistant?

Short answers

Yes, I have. | No, I haven't.
Yes, he has. | No, he hasn't.

Since October.
For about a year.

Statements

I've been waiting for a long time.
Lida has been waiting since 2:00.
We've been waiting all morning.

Time words

for (a long time)
since (2:00)
all (morning)

For a complete grammar chart and explanation, turn to page 149.

2 Practice

A Write. Complete the sentences. Use the present perfect continuous.

1. **A** How long ___has___ Talia ___been practicing___ for her driving test?
   (practice)

   B For about three months.

2. **A** _____ you _____ here for a long time?
   (work)

   B No, I haven't. I started six days ago.

3. **A** How long _____ Yin _____ for a job?
   (look)

   B Since last year.

4. **A** _____ Mr. Rivera _____ people all day?
   (interview)

   B Yes, he has.

5. **A** How long _____ you _____ to get an interview?
   (wait)

   B Since March.

6. **A** How long _____ they _____ to night school?
   (go)

   B All year.

Listen and check your answers. Then practice with a partner.

B **Talk** with a partner. Ask and answer questions.

> **A** How long has Sandra been talking on the phone?
> **B** For 20 minutes.

talk / for 20 minutes

wait / since 8:00

study / all morning

practice keyboarding / since 10:30

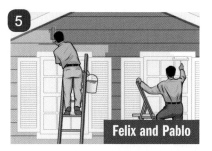

paint the house / for two days

work in the restaurant / since 1996

Write a sentence about each picture.

Sandra has been talking on the phone for 20 minutes.

3 Communicate

A **Talk** with your classmates. Find a person who does each activity. Ask how long the person has been doing it. Complete the chart.

> **A** Do you drive?
> **B** Yes, I do.

> **A** How long have you been driving?
> **B** For about six years. / Since 2002.

Name	Activity	How long?
Josefina	drive	*for six years / since 2002*
	cook for yourself	
	attend this school	
	work in this country	
	play soccer	
	use a computer	

B **Share** information about your classmates.

Phrasal verbs

1 Grammar focus: separable phrasal verbs

Statements

Alfred handed out the papers.

He handed the papers out.

He handed them out.

Common separable phrasal verbs

call back	hand out	turn down
clean up	put away / back	turn off
fill out	throw out / away	turn up

For a grammar explanation, turn to page 152.
For a list of phrasal verbs, turn to page 152.

2 Practice

A **Write.** Complete the sentences.

1

She's *handing out* papers.

She's *handing* the papers *out*.

She's *handing* them *out*.

2

He's _____ the cups.

He's *throwing* the cups *away*.

He's _____ them _____ .

3

He's _____ the volume.

He's _____ the volume _____ .

He's *turning* it *up*.

4

She's *filling out* a job application.

She's _____ the application _____ .

She's _____ it _____ .

Listen and check your answers.

B Talk with a partner. Make requests. Use the verbs in the box.

> **A** Please turn off the lights.
> **B** OK. I'll turn them off.

Useful language
lights → *them*
heat → *it*
Mr. Jones → *him*

call back	throw out
clean up	turn down
put away	turn off

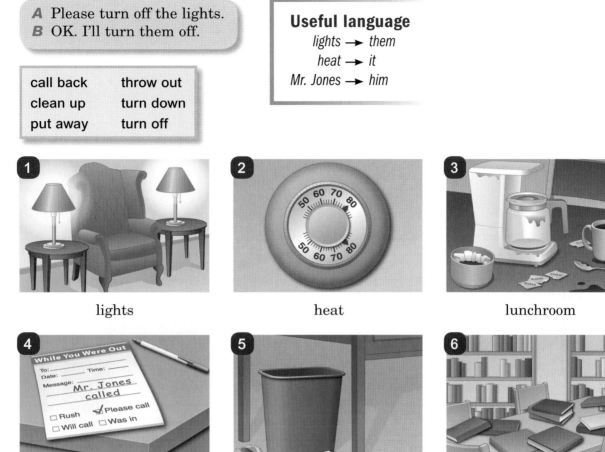

1. lights

2. heat

3. lunchroom

4. Mr. Jones

5. trash

6. books

Write sentences about each picture.

Please turn the lights off.

Useful language
To make a polite request, you can use:

Please . . .
Would you please . . . ?
Could you please . . . ?

3 Communicate

A Work in a small group. Ask and answer the questions.

1. Have you ever filled out an application form? Where? When?
2. Did you put anything away last night? What was it?
3. Is there someone you need to call back? Who?
4. What things do you want to throw away?
5. What things do you turn on, off, or up?
6. Is there anything you need to clean up? What is it?

B Share information about your classmates.

Reading

1 Before you read

Talk with your classmates. Answer the questions.

1. How many dates are in the reading? What are they?
2. What is the reading about?
3. What is a *blog*? Have you ever seen one?

2 Read

SELF-STUDY
AUDIO CD

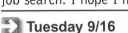 **Read** the blog. Listen and read again.

Scan the text for specific information. Read quickly to find dates. When you find the information you need, stop reading.

Blogland   <<Previous Blog   Next Blog >>   SEARCH

Eden's Blog

➜ Monday 9/15

Hello fellow job searchers! I have been looking for a job for several weeks. Everyone tells me that it's critical to network, so I've been telling everyone I know. I've been calling friends, relatives, and teachers to tell them about my job search. I hope I'll get a job interview!

➜ Tuesday 9/16

Today, I went to a job fair at my college. I filled out several applications and handed out some resumes. There were about 20 different companies there. Several of them said they were going to call me back. Wish me luck!

➜ Wednesday 9/24

I've been feeling depressed about the job search lately, but my counselor at school told me I shouldn't give up. He said I need to be patient. Today, I organized my papers. I made lists of the places I have applied to and the people I have talked to. I also did some more research online.

➜ Thursday 9/25

Great news! One of the companies from the job fair finally called me back! I've been preparing for the job interview all day. I'm really excited. I'm going to have a practice interview with some classmates today. That will prepare me for the real one.

➜ Monday 9/29

I had my interview today! I gave the interviewer a big smile and a firm handshake. I answered her questions with confidence. I'll let you know if I get the job. If you have any good job-searching tips, please share them with me!

3 After you read

A Scan the blog for Eden's activities. Match them with the dates.

1. Monday 9/15 _____   a. She had a practice interview with her classmates.
2. Tuesday 9/16 _____   b. She had a job interview.
3. Wednesday 9/24 _____   c. She organized her papers.
4. Thursday 9/25 _____   d. She's been telling everyone about her job search.
5. Monday 9/29 _____   e. She went to a job fair.

B Check your understanding.

1. Who wrote the blog?
2. How long has she been looking for a job?
3. Who did she network with?
4. How did she get a job interview?
5. How did she practice for the interview?

> **Culture note**
> *Blog* comes from the words *Web log*. Readers, or visitors, can write comments or just read.

C Build your vocabulary.

1. Read the dictionary entry for *critical*. How many definitions are there?

> **critical** */adj/* **1** saying that someone or something is bad or wrong **2** giving opinions on books, plays, films, etc. **3** very important; essential – **critically** */adv/*

2. Find the vocabulary in the reading. Underline the words. Find each word in a dictionary. Copy the part of speech and the definition that best fits the reading.

Vocabulary	Part of speech	Definition
1. critical	*adjective*	*very important; essential*
2. network		
3. fair		
4. patient		
5. firm		
6. confidence		

D Talk with a partner. Ask and answer the questions.

1. What is your most critical goal right now?
2. If you are trying to find a job, who can you network with?
3. How can you show confidence in a job interview?

1 Before you write

A Talk with a partner. Who do you send thank-you letters to? Make a list. Share your list with the class.

B Read the thank-you letter.

> 4 South Avenue, Apt. 303
> Kansas City, MO 64115
> September 30, 2008
>
> Janice Hill
> Personnel Manager
> Smart Shop
> 1255 Front Street
> Kansas City, MO 64114
>
> Dear Ms. Hill:
>
> I would like to thank you for the job interview I had with you on Monday, September 29th. I appreciate the time you spent with me. Thank you for showing me around the store and introducing me to some of the employees. I felt very comfortable with them.
>
> Thank you again for your time. I hope to hear from you soon.
>
> Sincerely,
> *Eden Babayan*
> Eden Babayan

Work with a partner. Answer the questions.

1. Who wrote the letter?
2. Who did she write it to?
3. What is the address of the writer?
4. What is the address of Ms. Hill?
5. What information is in the first sentence?
6. How many times did the writer say thank you?
7. How does the writer end the letter?

C Plan a formal thank-you letter. Complete the information.

Name and address of the person:

_____

_____

_____

Reason for saying thank you:

_____

_____

_____

Something specific you appreciate:

_____

_____

_____

2 Write

Write a thank-you letter to a person or a business. Use the letter in Exercise 1B and the information in Exercise 1C to help you.

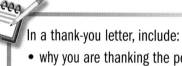

In a thank-you letter, include:
- why you are thanking the person
- what you appreciate
- another thank you at the end

3 After you write

A Check your writing.

	Yes	No
1. My first sentence says why I am thanking the person.	☐	☐
2. I mention something specific that I appreciated.	☐	☐
3. I thanked the person again at the end of the letter.	☐	☐

B Share your writing with a partner.

1. Take turns. Read your letter to a partner.
2. Comment on your partner's letter. Ask your partner a question about the letter. Tell your partner one thing you learned.

Lesson F *Another view*

1 Life-skills reading

Job Growth for Occupations Requiring an Associate's Degree or Vocational Training			
Occupation	2004	2014	Difference from 2004 to 2014
Registered nurses	2,394,000	3,096,000	+702,000
Nursing aides, orderlies, and attendants	1,455,000	1,781,000	+326,000
Automotive service technicians and mechanics	803,000	929,000	+126,000
Licensed practical and licensed vocational nurses	726,000	850,000	+124,000
Hairdressers, hairstylists, and cosmetologists	610,000	708,000	+98,000
Computer support specialists	518,000	638,000	+120,000
Preschool teachers (not special education)	431,000	573,000	+142,000

Source: *U.S. Department of Labor, Bureau of Labor Statistics, www.bls.gov/news.release/ooh.t01.htm*

A Read the questions. Look at the chart. Circle the answers.

1. What is *not* true about the jobs in the chart?
   a. They require an associate's degree.
   b. They require a bachelor's degree.
   c. They require vocational training.
   d. There will be more jobs in 2014 than in 2004.

2. Which occupation will grow the most from 2004 to 2014?
   a. automotive service technicians
   b. computer support specialists
   c. nursing aides
   d. registered nurses

3. What is the growth in number of jobs from 2004 to 2014 for hairdressers and cosmetologists?
   a. 98
   b. 980
   c. 9,800
   d. 98,000

4. This chart does *not* give information about _____ .
   a. automotive service technicians
   b. hairdressers and cosmetologists
   c. licensed vocational nurses
   d. special education teachers

B Talk with a partner. Ask and answer the questions.

1. What jobs are growing in your community? Are they the same as the jobs in the chart?
2. Is a job you want on this list? Is the number of jobs in this field growing?
3. Did anything in this chart surprise you? What was it?

106 Unit 8

2 Fun with language

A Talk with your classmates. Practice a job interview. Work in groups of three. Take turns playing each role.

Job interviewer: Ask the job applicant the questions.

Job applicant: Answer the interviewer's questions.

Observer: Watch and listen to the applicant. Take notes on the Observer's Sheet.

Job Interview Questions

a. What job are you applying for?
b. Tell me a little about your background.
c. Are you currently employed? If you are, tell me about your job.
d. What skills do you have that will help you in this job?
e. What are a few of your strengths?
f. Can you work any shift?
g. Several people have applied for this job. Why should I hire you?

> **Culture note**
> When you have a job interview, it is important to look the interviewer in the eye. Do not look up or away from him or her.

Observer's Sheet

What is the applicant's name?	
1. Did the applicant have good eye contact with the interviewer?	
2. Did the applicant speak slowly and clearly?	
3. Was the applicant enthusiastic?	
4. What are the applicant's skills?	
5. What are the applicant's personal strengths?	
6. Do you think this applicant should get the job? Why or why not?	

B Share information about the interview you observed. Use your notes from the Observer's Sheet.

3 Wrap up

Complete the **Self-assessment** on page 144.

Review

1 Listening

🔵 **Listen.** Put a check (✓) under the correct name.

	Clara	John
1. wants an SUV		✓
2. thinks a small car is better		
3. says an SUV is more comfortable		
4. wants to take friends for a ride		
5. wants to keep taking the bus		
6. wants to save money to buy a house		

Talk with a partner. Check your answers.

2 Grammar

A Write. Complete the story. Use the correct words.

Getting Work Experience

Hao ___*has been applying*___ for jobs as a computer technician since October.

1. will apply / has been applying

He _____ several interviews, but he hasn't gotten a job yet. He's

2. is having / has had

afraid of _____ again until he gets some experience. His friend

3. applying / apply

Terry gave him some good advice. He said Hao _____ think about

4. could / should

_____ at his son's school. Hao wants to call the school because the

5. volunteer / volunteering

school _____ problems with the computer system for a few months.

6. has been having / has

Hao is interested in _____ . It would be a win-win situation for both

7. help / helping

the school and Hao.

B Write. Look at the answers. Write the questions.

1. **A** Who _____ ?

   B Hao has been applying for a job.

2. **A** What _____ ?

   B He has been looking for a job as a computer technician.

3. **A** Where _____ ?

   B Hao wants to volunteer at his son's school.

Talk with a partner. Ask and answer the questions.

3 Pronunciation: linking sounds

A 💿 **Listen** to the phrasal verbs. Pay attention to the linking sounds.

1. clean up
2. think about
3. turn up
4. fill out
5. interested in
6. throw out
7. put on
8. tired of

💿 **Listen again and repeat.**

B 💿 **Listen and repeat.** Pay attention to the linking sounds in the phrasal verbs.

1. **A** What do you need to do?
   B I have to clean up the kitchen.
   A Can I help?
   B Sure. Could you throw out the trash?
   A I'd be happy to.

2. **A** Don't you think it's cold in here?
   B It's a little cold.
   A Why don't you turn up the heat?
   B That costs too much money. You can put on my jacket.

C **Talk** with a partner. Practice the conversations. Pay attention to the linking sounds in the phrasal verbs.

1. **A** Do you need some help?
   B I'm interested in applying for a job here.
   A OK. Just fill out this application and return it to me.
   B Thanks.
   A Don't forget to put your name on it.

2. **A** May I help you?
   B I may be interested in buying a big-screen TV.
   A We have some great deals. Let me show you.
   B Thanks, but I'd like to just look around some more.

3. **A** Do you want to go to a movie tonight?
   B What do you think about just staying home?
   A That's fine. There's a good game on TV.
   B OK. First help me clean up the kitchen. Then we can watch the game.

4. **A** I want to register for English classes.
   B Fill out this form, please.
   A Can you help me?
   B Sure. I just need to put away these papers.
   A Thank you.

D **Write** four questions. Use the words in Exercise 3A. Ask your partner. Remember to connect the sounds.

Did you clean up the kitchen last night?

1. _____
2. _____
3. _____
4. _____

Get ready

1 Talk about the pictures

A What do you see?
B What is happening?
C What's the story?

2 Listening

SELF-STUDY
AUDIO CD

A 🔊 **Listen** and answer the questions.

1. Who are the speakers?
2. What are they talking about?

SELF-STUDY
AUDIO CD

B 🔊 **Listen again.** Take notes. Answer the questions.

1. What happened at Monica's house?	*someone broke into her house*
2. How did the robber get in?	
3. What did the robber steal?	
4. How has the neighborhood changed?	
5. What did Samantha use to do with the front door?	
6. What does Samantha think they should do?	

Listen again. Check your answers.

SELF-STUDY
AUDIO CD

C 🔊 **Read.** Complete the story. Listen and check your answers.

broke into	come over	crime	got in	mess	robbed	robber	stole

Monica calls her friend Samantha with bad news. While Monica and

her husband were at a neighbor's house, someone ___broke into___ their home
                                                        1

and _____ their TV, DVD player, jewelry, and some cash. Monica is
          2

upset because the _____ took her mother's ring. She says the person
                        3

_____ through a window in the back bedroom.
      4

Samantha is worried. She says they never used to have so much

_____ in their neighborhood. She tells Monica that last week someone
      5

_____ their neighbor Mr. Purdy, too. Samantha thinks they should
      6

start a Neighborhood Watch program. Monica agrees, but first, she needs to

clean up the _____ in her house. Samantha offers to _____
                  7   8

and help.

D **Talk** with a partner.

Tell about a crime that happened to you or someone you know.

Past continuous

1 Grammar focus: questions and answers

Questions	Answers	
What was Beth doing yesterday morning? What were the neighbors doing at 10:00?	She was cleaning her house. They were watching TV.	
Was Maria visiting a neighbor last night? Were they watching a movie at 8:30?	Yes, she was. Yes, they were.	No, she wasn't. No, they weren't.

For a complete grammar chart and explanation, turn to page 150.

2 Practice

A Write. Complete the sentences. Use the past continuous.

What were you doing at 8:30 last night?

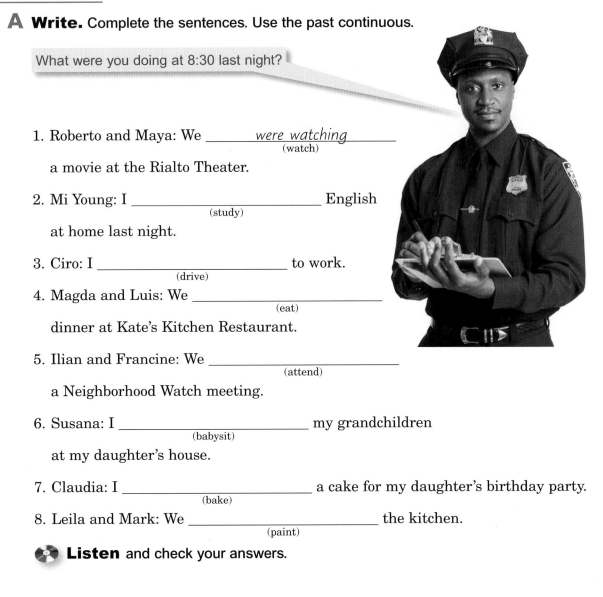

1. Roberto and Maya: We _____*were watching*_____
   (watch)
   a movie at the Rialto Theater.

2. Mi Young: I _____ English
   (study)
   at home last night.

3. Ciro: I _____ to work.
   (drive)

4. Magda and Luis: We _____
   (eat)
   dinner at Kate's Kitchen Restaurant.

5. Ilian and Francine: We _____
   (attend)
   a Neighborhood Watch meeting.

6. Susana: I _____ my grandchildren
   (babysit)
   at my daughter's house.

7. Claudia: I _____ a cake for my daughter's birthday party.
   (bake)

8. Leila and Mark: We _____ the kitchen.
   (paint)

   Listen and check your answers.

B Talk with a partner. Look at the picture. Ask and answer questions. Use the past continuous and the verbs in the box.

> **A** What was the father doing at 7:00 p.m.?
> **B** He was reading.

| knit | play cards | read | sew | sleep | talk | watch TV |

Write a sentence about each person.

The father was reading.

3 Communicate

A Work in a small group. Ask and answer questions. Take notes in the chart.

> **A** Sergio, were you at home at 9:00 a.m. yesterday?
> **B** Yes, I was.
> **A** What were you doing?
> **B** I was sleeping.

Name	Time	Action
Sergio	9:00 a.m.	sleeping

B Share information about your classmates.

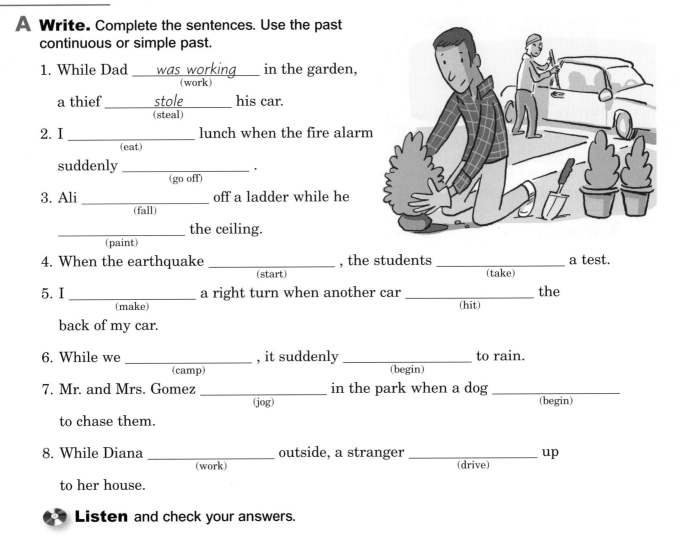

Lesson C *Past continuous and simple past*

1 Grammar focus: *when* and *while*

While Maxine and Joel were sleeping, a fire started in the kitchen.
When the fire started, Maxine and Joel were sleeping.

A fire started in the kitchen while Maxine and Joel were sleeping.
Maxine and Joel were sleeping when the fire started.

For a grammar explanation, turn to page 153.

2 Practice

A Write. Complete the sentences. Use the past continuous or simple past.

1. While Dad ___*was working*___ in the garden,
   (work)
   a thief _____*stole*_____ his car.
   (steal)

2. I _____ lunch when the fire alarm
   (eat)
   suddenly _____ .
   (go off)

3. Ali _____ off a ladder while he
   (fall)
   _____ the ceiling.
   (paint)

4. When the earthquake _____ , the students _____ a test.
   (start)   (take)

5. I _____ a right turn when another car _____ the
   (make)   (hit)
   back of my car.

6. While we _____ , it suddenly _____ to rain.
   (camp)   (begin)

7. Mr. and Mrs. Gomez _____ in the park when a dog _____
   (jog)   (begin)
   to chase them.

8. While Diana _____ outside, a stranger _____ up
   (work)   (drive)
   to her house.

🔘 **Listen** and check your answers.

114 Unit 9

B **Talk** with a partner. Look at the pictures. Ask and answer questions. Use *when* or *while*.

> **A** What happened?
> **B** While the woman was working, a tree fell on her house.

work   fall   drive   run out of gas

eat   get a parking ticket   cook dinner   the lights go out

Write sentences about what happened.

The woman was working when a tree fell on her house.

3 Communicate

A **Work** with a partner. Describe a situation that happened to you. Answer the questions.

1. What happened?
2. When and where did it happen?
3. What were you doing when it happened?

B **Share** information about your partner.

Lesson D Reading

1 Before you read

Look at the picture. Answer the questions.

1. Who are the people in the picture?
2. What do you think is happening?
3. How do they probably feel?

2 Read

SELF-STUDY
AUDIO CD

Read the newspaper article.
Listen and read again.

Home Is More Than a Building

A few months ago, Pedro Ramirez, 45, lost his job in a grocery store. To pay the bills, he got a part-time job at night. Several days later, Pedro's wife, Luisa, gave him a big surprise. She was pregnant with their sixth child. Pedro was happy but worried. "How am I going to support another child without a full-time job?" he wondered.

That evening, Pedro and Luisa got some more news. A fire was coming near their home. By the next morning, the fire was very close. The police ordered every family in the neighborhood to evacuate. The Ramirez family moved quickly. While Pedro was gathering their legal documents, Luisa grabbed the family photographs, and the children put their pets – a cat and a bird – in the family's truck. Then, the family drove to the home of their eldest daughter, one hour away.

About 24 hours later, Pedro and Luisa got very bad news. The fire destroyed their home. They lost almost everything. With no home, only part-time work, and a baby coming, Pedro was even more worried about the future.

For the next three months, the Ramirez family stayed with their daughter while workers were rebuilding their home. Many generous people helped them during that difficult time. Friends took them shopping for clothes. Strangers left gifts at their door. A group of children collected $500 to buy bicycles for the Ramirez children.

Because of all the help from friends and neighbors, the Ramirez family was able to rebuild their lives. Two months after the fire, Luisa mailed out holiday cards with this message: "Home is more than a building. Home is wherever there is love."

In a story, time phrases show changes in time.

A few months ago, . . .
Several days later, . . .
That evening, . . .

3 After you read

A Check your understanding.

Scan the reading. Look for the time phrases. Write numbers to show the order of events.

_1_ Pedro lost his job.

____ Luisa mailed out holiday cards.

____ The fire destroyed Pedro and Luisa's home.

____ Pedro and Luisa heard about the fire near their home.

____ The police ordered people in the neighborhood to evacuate.

____ Luisa told Pedro she was pregnant.

____ The Ramirez family stayed with their daughter for three months.

B Build your vocabulary.

Find the words in the story, and underline them. Circle the definitions that best match the reading.

1. support
   a. pay for necessary things
   b. help
   c. say that you agree with someone

2. evacuate
   a. clean
   b. go inside a house
   c. leave a dangerous place

3. gathering
   a. a meeting of people
   b. a group of things
   c. collecting

4. grabbed
   a. took quickly
   b. held someone with force
   c. stole

5. destroyed
   a. broke completely
   b. killed
   c. hurt

6. generous
   a. critical
   b. helpful
   c. sad

7. strangers
   a. family
   b. friends
   c. people you don't know

8. message
   a. medical treatment
   b. information you send
   c. a person who brings things

C Talk with a partner. Ask and answer the questions.

1. Tell about a time when people had to evacuate their homes. What happened?
2. Has someone been generous to you or your family? How?
3. How do you feel about accepting help from strangers?

1 Before you write

A Talk with a partner. Think about an emergency. Answer the questions.

1. **Who** did it happen to?
2. **What** happened?
3. **When** did it happen?
4. **Where** did it happen?
5. **Why** or **how** did it happen?

B Read the story.

Fire!

One evening last summer, my husband and I were preparing dinner together. My husband was cooking outside, and I was setting the table inside. Suddenly, my husband ran into the kitchen and shouted, "There's a fire in the backyard!" I ran outside and saw fire in the bushes next to our fence. I was really scared because my 70-year-old parents live next door. Luckily, my husband acted quickly. He called the fire department and then started putting water on the fire. The firefighters arrived quickly, and they easily put out the fire. They said a coal from the barbecue started it.

My parents were very surprised when they saw the firefighters. They were watching the news in the living room, and they never knew there was a problem. My father said, "Let's go back and watch the news. Maybe we're on TV!"

Work with a partner. Answer the questions.

1. Who is the story about?
2. When did it happen?
3. Where did it happen?
4. What were the people doing when the story started?
5. What was the emergency?
6. Why was the writer scared?
7. How did the story end?

C Write a plan for a story about an emergency that happened to you or someone you know. Answer the questions.

1. Who is the story about?	
2. Where did it happen?	
3. When did it happen?	
4. What were the people doing when the story started?	
5. What was the emergency?	
6. How did the story end?	

2 Write

Write a story about an emergency that happened to you or someone you know. Use the information from Exercises 1B and 1C to help you.

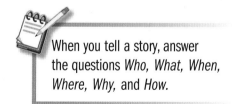

When you tell a story, answer the questions *Who, What, When, Where, Why,* and *How.*

3 After you write

A Check your writing.

	Yes	No
1. I gave my story a title.	☐	☐
2. My story answers the questions *Who, What, When, Where, Why,* and *How.*	☐	☐
3. I used the past continuous with *when* and *while* correctly.	☐	☐

B Share your writing with a partner.

1. Take turns. Read your story to a partner.
2. Comment on your partner's story. Ask your partner a question about the story. Tell your partner one thing you learned.

Another view

1 Life-skills reading

Rank	Safest States in 2006
1	North Dakota
2	Maine
3	Vermont
4	New Hampshire
5	Wyoming
19	New Jersey
20	New York
32	Illinois
40	Texas
41	California
44	Florida

Rank	Safest States in 2007
1	North Dakota
2	Vermont
3	Maine
4	New Hampshire
5	Wyoming
18	New Jersey
20	New York
30	Illinois
39	Texas
42	California
43	Florida

Source: *Crime State Rankings 2007*

A Read the questions. Look at the charts. Circle the answers.

1. Which state had the same rank in 2006 and 2007?
   a. Florida
   b. Illinois
   c. New Jersey
   d. New York

2. Which state had a different rank in 2006 and 2007?
   a. New Hampshire
   b. North Dakota
   c. Vermont
   d. Wyoming

3. Which state became safer in 2007?
   a. California
   b. Illinois
   c. Maine
   d. Wyoming

4. Which state became less safe in 2007?
   a. California
   b. New Jersey
   c. Texas
   d. Vermont

B Talk with your classmates. Ask and answer the questions.

1. Do you feel safe where you live? Why?
2. Where do you think is the safest place to live?
3. Where do you think is the most dangerous place to live?

2 Fun with language

A **Work** with a partner. Ask questions about the safety items in the photos. Complete the chart.

> Does the school have a fire extinguisher?

> How many fire extinguishers are there? Where are they?

		Yes	No	How many?	Location(s)
1 fire extinguisher					
2 emergency-exit map	Fire-escape routes You are here				
3 smoke alarm					
4 fire alarm	FIRE				
5 first-aid kit					
6 emergency-exit signs	EXIT				

B **Share** your information with the class. Discuss the questions.

1. Which items does your school have?
2. Which items does it need to have?
3. Which items do you have at home?
4. Which items do you have at work?

3 Wrap up

Complete the **Self-assessment** on page 145.

Get ready

1 Talk about the pictures

A What do you see?
B What is happening?
C What's the story?

Leisure

2 Listening

SELF-STUDY AUDIO CD **A** **Listen** and answer the questions.

1. Who are the speakers?
2. What are they talking about?

SELF-STUDY AUDIO CD **B** **Listen again.** Complete the chart.

	San Francisco	Camping
Transportation	Round-trip airfare per person: $_____	Gas for the car: $_____
Lodging	Hotel room per night: $_____ Room tax per night: _____%	Campsite per night: $_____

Listen again. Check your answers.

SELF-STUDY AUDIO CD **C** **Read.** Complete the story. Listen and check your answers.

book a flight	days off	reserve	tax
camping	discounts	round-trip	tourist

Felicia is exhausted. She needs a vacation. Her husband, Ricardo, says maybe he can ask his boss for a few _____*days off*_____ . Felicia says she would like to go
₁
to San Francisco. She and her husband look for special travel _____
₂
on the Internet. If they _____ at least seven days ahead, they can get
₃
a _____ ticket for less than $100. On the other hand, hotel room rates
₄
will be high because summer is the most popular _____ season. Also,
₅
there is a room _____ on hotel rooms in San Francisco. They figure
₆
out that a three-day trip to San Francisco will cost almost $900.

Felicia and her husband decide to change their plans. If they go

_____ , they will save a lot of money and their daughter will have
₇
more fun. Felicia's husband will _____ the campsite after he talks to
₈
his boss.

Culture note
Advertisements for hotels do not include the room tax. The tax adds 7% to 16% per night to the cost of the room.

D **Talk** with a partner. Answer the question.

Which would you prefer: a trip to San Francisco or camping in the mountains?

Dependent clauses

1 Grammar focus: clauses with *if*

> If the fare is cheap enough, we will fly.
> If the weather is bad, she won't go swimming.

> We will fly if the fare is cheap enough.
> She won't go swimming if the weather is bad.

For a grammar explanation, turn to page 153.

2 Practice

A Write. Complete the sentences. Use the simple present or future form of the verbs.

1. Annette and William _____*will take*_____ their children to Sea Adventure
   (take)

   next month if William _____*gets*_____ a few days off.
   (get)

2. If they _____ a discount, they _____ a room
   (get)   (reserve)

   at a hotel.

3. If prices _____ too high, they _____ an
   (be)   (not / take)

   expensive vacation.

4. We _____ a picnic on Saturday if it _____ .
   (have)   (not / rain)

5. If you _____ me the money, I _____ the
   (give)   (buy)

   concert tickets.

6. If you _____ to Chicago, we _____ you at
   (come)   (meet)

   the airport.

7. They _____ to Miami next month if they _____
   (fly)   (find)

   a cheap flight.

8. We _____ camping if the weather _____ too hot.
   (not / go)   (be)

🔘 **Listen** and check your answers.

B Talk with a partner. Ask and answer questions about the pictures.

> **A** What will John do if the weather is good?
> **B** He'll play soccer.

> **A** What will he do if the weather isn't good?
> **B** He'll watch a movie.

1. play soccer — watch a movie

2. Melinda and Pedro — go hiking — go shopping

3. Ken — go swimming — clean the house

4. Andrea — work in the garden — read a book

Write a sentence about each picture.

If the weather is good, John will play soccer.
He'll watch a movie if the weather isn't good.

3 Communicate

A Work with a partner. Ask and answer questions. Take notes in the chart.

> **A** What will you do if you have time off in the summer?
> **B** I'll visit my family in Mexico.

1. have time off in the summer	*visit family in Mexico*
2. have a three-day weekend	
3. get some extra money	
4. the weather is beautiful next weekend	

B Share information about your partner.

Lesson C *Dependent clauses*

1 Grammar focus: *before* and *after* with future meaning

> After Kim finishes school, he will take a vacation.
> Before Kim takes a vacation, he will finish school.

> Kim will take a vacation after he finishes school.
> Kim will finish school before he takes a vacation.

For a grammar explanation, turn to page 153.

2 Practice

A Write. Complete the sentences. Use the correct form of the verb.

1. Kara ____will talk____ (talk) to a travel agent before she ____books____ (book) a flight.

2. Before Cynthia _____ (leave) for Puerto Rico, she _____ (buy) some new clothes.

3. Donald _____ (take) a taxi to the hotel after he _____ (pick up) his baggage.

4. The campers _____ (make) a fire before they _____ (cook) their dinner.

5. After they _____ (finish) eating, they _____ (clean up) the campsite.

6. I _____ (call) you after I _____ (return) from my trip.

7. After I _____ (get) my passport, I _____ (make) the reservations.

8. Before we _____ (go) to Mexico, we _____ (learn) some words in Spanish

9. Kim _____ (lock) the doors before he _____ (leave) for the airport.

Listen and check your answers.

126   Unit 10

B **Talk** with a partner. Anita is going to the airport. Talk about her plans. Use *before* or *after*.

> *A* After Anita checks in, she'll go through security.
> *B* Before Anita goes through security, she'll check in.

check in

go through security

buy a cup of coffee

read a newspaper

get on the plane

turn off her cell phone

Write sentences about Anita. Use *before* and *after*.

Anita will go through security after she checks in.

3 Communicate

A **Imagine** you are going to take a weekend trip. Choose the location. Write three things you need to do before the trip.

B **Interview** a partner. Take notes in the chart.

> *A* Where will you go on your trip?
> *B* To the mountains.

> *A* What will you do first?
> *B* I'll reserve a campsite.

> *A* What will you do after you reserve a campsite?
> *B* I'll pack warm clothes.

C **Share** information about your partner.

You
Location:
1.
2.
3.

Your partner
Location:
1.
2.
3.

Lesson **D** *Reading*

1 Before you read

Look at the picture. Answer the questions.

1. What do you see on the postcard?
2. Would you like to visit this place? Why or why not?

2 Read

 SELF-STUDY AUDIO CD

Read the article from a tourist guide. Listen and read again.

San Francisco

THE ROCK San Francisco's Biggest Tourist Attraction

Alcatraz, a small, rocky island in the middle of San Francisco Bay, was once the most famous prison in the United States. For a period of 29 years, from 1934 to 1963, over 1,500 dangerous criminals lived in the prison's 378 cells. People believed that it was impossible to escape from Alcatraz Island. However, in 1962 two brothers, John and Clarence Anglin, and another man named Frank Morris escaped on a raft made of raincoats. A famous movie, *Escape from Alcatraz*, tells this amazing story. Other famous prisoners who lived on the island included Al Capone, the gangster, and Robert Stroud, the "Birdman of Alcatraz."

Alcatraz prison closed in 1963. The island became a national park, and since then, it has been a major attraction for tourists from all over the world. These days, many people call Alcatraz by its popular name, "The Rock."

In the summer, it is wise to buy tickets to the island in advance because the ferries sell out. Evening tours are less crowded. The admission prices listed include the ferry, tickets, and an audio tour.

General admission	
Adult (18–61)	$24.50
Junior (12–17)	$24.50
Child (5–11)	$15.25
Senior (62+)	$23.25

Words between commas sometimes explain the words before them.

For a period of 29 years, ***from 1934 to 1963,*** *. . .*

3 After you read

A Check your understanding.

1. What is Alcatraz?
2. Why did dangerous criminals go to Alcatraz?
3. What happened in 1962?
4. How long has Alcatraz been a tourist attraction?
5. How much is admission for a ten-year-old child?
6. If an adult wants to go on a tour, how much will it cost?

B Build your vocabulary.

1. Find the following words in the reading. Underline them.

attraction	cells	in advance	sell out
prison	escape	ferries	admission

2. Work with a partner. Guess the meaning of the words. Find the clues that helped you. Then use a dictionary to check your guesses.

> I guess that *attraction* means a place tourists want to visit. My clue was the phrase "biggest tourist attraction" in the title. The dictionary definition of *attraction [noun]* is "a thing or place that tourists like to see or visit."

3. Complete the sentences. Use the words from Exercise B1.

a. The Empire State Building in New York is a famous tourist _____ .

b. General _____ to the museum is $24.50 for adults.

c. Tickets to popular music concerts often _____ very quickly.

d. We bought our tickets six months _____ .

e. To get to the Ellis Island Immigration Museum in New York, you have to take one of the _____ from Manhattan.

f. Alcatraz used to be a _____ . Then it became a national park.

g. Each prisoner in Alcatraz lived in one of the 378 _____ .

h. Thirty-six men tried to _____ from Alcatraz.

C Talk with a partner. Ask and answer the questions.

1. Tell about a popular tourist attraction in a city you have visited. What was the cost of admission?
2. What kinds of tickets do you usually buy in advance?
3. Have you ever taken a ferry ride? Where did you go?

 *Writing*

1 Before you write

A **Work** with a partner. Write the name of a tourist attraction in your community. Make a list of things to do or see there.

Attraction: _____

1. _____

2. _____

3. _____

4. _____

B **Read** the paragraph.

The San Diego County Fair

One of the biggest tourist attractions in San Diego is the San Diego County Fair. It is open from June 15 to July 4. The fair has something for everyone. It has a beautiful flower show and a photography exhibit. If you have children, they will love the Ferris wheel and the fast rides. If you like animals, you can watch many different animal competitions. The winner in each competition gets a blue ribbon. The fair also has displays of new products, such as cleaning products and cooking tools. When you get hungry, you can buy food from at least 25 different booths. After you have eaten dinner, you can listen to a concert of live music until late in the evening. The fair ends with spectacular fireworks on Independence Day, the 4th of July.

C Complete the outline. Write five examples of things to do at the San Diego County Fair.

Main idea: *The fair has something for everyone.*
Examples:

1. _____

_____

2. _____

_____

3. _____

_____

4. _____

_____

5. _____

_____

> Use complex sentences to make your writing more interesting.
>
> *If you have children, they will love the Ferris wheel and the fast rides.*
>
> *When you get hungry, you can buy food from at least 25 different booths.*

Conclusion: *The fair ends with fireworks on the 4th of July.*

D Work with a partner. Look at Exercise 1B. Find four complex sentences. Underline them.

2 Write

Write a paragraph about a tourist attraction in your city. Before you write, make an outline. Use Exercises 1B and 1C to help you. Include the main idea, conclusion, and at least three examples.

3 After you write

A Check your writing.

	Yes	No
1. My paragraph has a main idea and a conclusion.	☐	☐
2. My paragraph has at least three examples.	☐	☐
3. My paragraph has complex sentences with *before, after, when,* or *if.*	☐	☐

B Share your writing with a partner.

1. Take turns. Read your paragraph to a partner.
2. Comment on your partner's paragraph. Ask your partner a question about the paragraph. Tell your partner one thing you learned.

1 Life-skills reading

Gateway Inn
524 Memorial Highway
Orlando, Florida
407-555-7000

Amenities	Restaurant in lobby (kids eat free), outdoor pool, fitness center, golf nearby, free transportation to local theme parks
Distance from destinations	Theme parks (3.5 miles)
Room rates	Budget: $69–$79 Standard rooms: $100–$132 Deluxe: $149–$200
Room tax	12%

Western Universal Inn
4617 Southland Rd.
Orlando, Florida
407-555-9100

Amenities	Breakfast buffet, outdoor pool, self-parking (free), in-room safe, iron, hair dryer, Internet access
Distance from destinations	Daytona Beach (47 miles), International Drive (1 mile), Winter Park (8 miles), theme parks (12 miles)
Room rates	Budget: $100–$125 Standard rooms: $120–$145 Deluxe: $150–$200
Room tax	12%

A **Read** the questions. Look at the hotel information. Circle the answers.

1. What is the rate for a standard room at the Gateway Inn?
   a. $69–$79
   b. $100–$132
   c. $120–$145
   d. $149–$200

2. Where can children eat for free?
   a. Daytona Beach
   b. Gateway Inn
   c. Western Universal Inn
   d. none of the above

3. How far is the Western Universal Inn from theme parks?
   a. 3.5 miles
   b. 8 miles
   c. 10 miles
   d. 12 miles

4. Where is self-parking free?
   a. Gateway Inn
   b. Western Universal Inn
   c. neither *a* nor *b*
   d. both *a* and *b*

B **Talk** with a partner. Ask and answer the questions.

Which hotel do you prefer? Why?

2 Fun with language

A Imagine your "dream" vacation. You will have as much money as you want to spend. You can go anywhere in the world. Write short answers to the questions.

1. Where will you go?	
2. Who will you go with?	
3. What time of year will you go there?	
4. How will you get there?	
5. Where will you stay?	
6. How long will you stay?	
7. What will you do before you leave?	
8. What will you do and see there?	
9. What will you bring back?	

B Talk in small groups. Tell about your dream vacation.

3 Wrap up

Complete the **Self-assessment** on page 145.

Review

1 Listening

🔘 **Listen.** Put a check (✓) under *Yes* or *No*.

	Yes	No
1. Brad Spencer was missing for two nights.	☐	☑
2. He disappeared Sunday.	☐	☐
3. He was camping with his friends.	☐	☐
4. He was wearing only a T-shirt and shorts.	☐	☐
5. When the park police found him, he was playing his guitar.	☐	☐
6. If Brad returns to the park, he's going to stay on the trails.	☐	☐

Talk with a partner. Check your answers.

2 Grammar

A Write. Complete the story. Use the correct words.

A Problem in Chicago

Tina Foster is visiting Chicago for the first time. While she _____*was taking*_____
1. took / was taking

a walk in Lincoln Park early this morning, she _____ her wallet with
2. lost / was losing

all her cash, identification, and credit cards. When she got back to her hotel, she

realized that her wallet _____ . She is going to _____
3. missed / was missing   4. search / searching

the park. If she _____ her wallet, she _____ the credit
5. doesn't find / didn't find   6. calls / will call

card companies. After she _____ her credit cards, she
7. cancels / canceled

_____ to the nearest police station and file a police report.
8. will go / goes

B Write. Look at the answers. Write the questions.

1. **A** Who _____ ?

   B Tina Foster is visiting Chicago for the first time.

2. **A** What _____ ?

   B Tina was taking a walk when she lost her wallet.

3. **A** Where _____ ?

   B She will file a police report at the nearest police station.

Talk with a partner. Ask and answer the questions.

3 Pronunciation: unstressed vowel

A 🔊 **Listen** to the unstressed vowel sound in these words. Unstressed vowels sound like "uh."

1. up-sét
2. a-bóut
3. fá-mi-ly
4. éx-tra
5. trá-vel

6. po-líce
7. va-cá-tion
8. dán-ge-rous
9. Sa-mán-tha
10. phó-to-graphs

> The unstressed vowels are in green.

🔊 **Listen again and repeat.**

B 🔊 **Listen and repeat.** Then underline the unstressed vowels in these words.

1. Samantha is upset.
2. Where's the travel agent?
3. The prison is dangerous.
4. It's about seven o'clock.

5. Did you take photographs?
6. Call the police!
7. She'll think about visiting her family.
8. I need a vacation.

Talk with a partner. Compare your answers.

C **Talk** with a partner. Practice the conversations. Pay attention to the unstressed vowel sounds in green.

1. **A** There was a lot of excitement at the Community Adult School yesterday!
   B What are you talking about?
   A There was a fire in the kitchen!
   B Did the fire department come?
   A Yes. A student heard the smoke alarm and called 911 right away.

2. **A** Betty is going to Washington next week!
   B Are you serious? Won't that cost a lot?
   A Well, she probably got a cheap ticket.
   B Is she traveling with her family?
   A No. Her husband's going to take care of the children.

D **Write** five questions. Use the words in Exercise 3A. Ask your partner. Remember to pay attention to the unstressed vowel sound.

What makes you get upset?

1. _____
2. _____
3. _____
4. _____
5. _____

Personality types

A Use the Internet.

Find a free personality survey.
Take the survey.
Copy or print out the results.

Keywords personality surveys

B Make a chart.

Write three things about your
personality from the survey.
Do you agree or disagree with
the survey? Check (✓) your answer.

	Agree	Disagree
I like to be with people.	✓	
I like to think about the future.		✓
I like to talk about my feelings.	✓	

C Share your information.

Show your chart to your classmates.
Talk about the survey.

Strategies for learning English

A Make a list.

What are some strategies you have used to learn English?
Share your strategies with a partner.

B Make a chart.

Write some strategies you want
to try.
Set goals. When will you start
using these strategies?

Strategy	Goal
Write new words in my notebook.	after class
Listen to English on the radio.	tonight
Talk to my neighbors.	this weekend

C Share your information.

Talk to your classmates about your strategies.
Make a class booklet of learning strategies.

Volunteer opportunities

A Use the Internet.

Find information about a place to volunteer in your city.
Write the names of three places.

Keywords (your city), volunteer opportunities

B Take notes. Answer these questions.

1. Where can you volunteer?
2. What can you do there?
3. What is the telephone number?

Name	Volunteer work	Telephone number
Senior Center	deliver meals	555-3068
Heart Hospital	greet visitors	555-4752
Brown Elementary School	help students do their homework	555-4231

C Share your information.

Tell your class about the places and the volunteer work.
How many classmates want to volunteer? Where do they want to volunteer?

Health Tips

A Make a list.

Write three ways to stay healthy.

Ways to stay healthy:
Exercise.
Eat well.
Get plenty of sleep.

B Make a chart.

Write three ways to stay healthy.
Write examples of these three ways.

Ways to stay healthy	Examples
Exercise.	walk, run, swim, ride a bike
Eat well.	eat fresh fruit and vegetables, drink lots of water
Get plenty of sleep.	go to bed early

C Share your information.

Talk about your ideas.
Make a class poster.
What are the best ideas?
Take a class vote.

Weekend activities

A Use the Internet.

Find the entertainment section of your local newspaper online.
Find information about weekend activities in your city.

Keywords | (name of your local newspaper), entertainment

B Take notes. Answer these questions.

1. What is the activity?
2. When is the activity?
3. Where is the activity?

Activity	When	Where
Jazz concert	Thursday: 8:00 p.m.	Town Park
Garden show	Saturday and Sunday: 9:00 a.m.–9:00 p.m.	Civic Center
Art show	Friday: 10:00 a.m.–5:00 p.m.	15 Main Street

C Share your information.

Tell your classmates about the activities.
Make a class wall chart of weekend activities.
Discuss with your classmates. Who would like to go to each activity?

Tips for managing time

A Make a list.

What are ways to manage your study time?
Write three ideas.

1. Find a quiet and comfortable place to study.
2. Decide what time of day is best for you to study.
3. Make a list of what you have to study.

B Interview your classmates.

Find two more ways to manage study time. Write them in your chart.

C Share your information.

Make a class wall chart.
Talk about ways to manage your study time.

Shopping

A Think about shopping.

What do you want to buy?

Choose one: a car, a computer, a big-screen TV, furniture, or appliances.

B Find an ad.

Find an ad from two different stores for the item you want to buy.

Look in this week's paper. Look in the mail for a flyer. Look on TV.

C Make a chart.

Write information about your ads.
Write the name of the item.
Write the name of the stores.
Write the price of the item in each store.

Item	Sam's TV Discount Store	A & B Electronics
TV	$2,900.00	$3,100.00

D Share your information.

Find a picture of the item you want to buy.
Paste it on a piece of paper.
Write the price and any other information you find.
Show it to the class, and compare stores.

Job interview

A Use the Internet.

Find common interview questions.

> interview questions

What experience do you have?
What are your goals?
Do you have any questions?

B Make a chart.

Write some interview questions.

C Answer the questions.

Write your answers.

Questions	Answers
What experience do you have?	I've been a salesperson for ten years.
What are your goals?	I'd like to be a manager. I enjoy working with people.
Do you have any questions?	Yes. When can I start?

D Share your information.

Show your questions and answers to a partner.
Tell the class about your partner.

Projects

Home safety

A Think about your house or apartment.

Check (✓) the things you have.
Answer the questions.

	How many?	Where?
☐ fire extinguisher		
☐ smoke alarm		
☐ fire alarm		
☐ first-aid kit		
☐ other:		

B Make a list.

Write things you need for your
house or apartment.

> fire alarm
> other: evacuation plan

C Share your information.

Talk with your classmates.
Make a list of important safety items for the home.

Hotel search

A Use the Internet.

Find information about a hotel in your city or a city you would like to visit.
If possible, print pictures of the hotel.

> (city name), hotels

B Make a chart.

Write the name of the hotel.
Write the address.
Write other information.

Name	Address	Telephone	Rates	Other
Hilltop Hotel	87 Hilltop Road San Antonio, TX	210-555-8376	$79.00–$109.00	free breakfast pool parking: $5.00 a day

C Share your information.

Make a poster about your hotel.
Show your poster to your class.
Talk about the different hotels.
Where would the class like to stay? Take a class vote.

Self-assessments

Unit 1 Personal information

A Vocabulary Write eight new words you have learned.

_____   _____   _____   _____

_____   _____   _____   _____

B Skills and functions Read the sentences. Rate yourself. Circle 3 (*I agree.*) OR
2 (*I'm not sure.*) OR 1 (*I can't do this.*).

I can ask and answer questions using verbs + gerunds: *Do you enjoy **dancing**? I love **dancing**.*	3 2 1
I can use **more than**, **less than**, and **as much as** to compare likes and interests: *I like reading **more than** watching TV.*	3 2 1
I can predict what I am going to read by looking at the title and pictures.	3 2 1
I can write a paragraph describing my personality and right job.	3 2 1
I can read and understand a personal ad.	3 2 1

C What's next? Choose one.

☐ I am ready for the unit test.   ☐ I need more practice with _____ .

Unit 2 At school

A Vocabulary Write eight new words you have learned.

_____   _____   _____   _____

_____   _____   _____   _____

B Skills and functions Read the sentences. Rate yourself. Circle 3 (*I agree.*) OR
2 (*I'm not sure.*) OR 1 (*I can't do this.*).

I can ask and answer present perfect questions with **How long, for,** and **since**: **How long has** he **been** here? He **has been** here **for two years** / **since January**.	3 2 1
I can ask and answer present perfect questions with **ever**: *Have you **ever** studied French? No, I haven't.*	3 2 1
I can find examples in a reading.	3 2 1
I can write a paragraph about my learning strategies.	3 2 1
I can read and understand a list of tips for taking tests.	3 2 1

C What's next? Choose one.

☐ I am ready for the unit test.   ☐ I need more practice with _____ .

Unit 3 Friends and family

A Vocabulary Write eight new words you have learned.

_____ _____ _____ _____

_____ _____ _____ _____

B Skills and functions Read the sentences. Rate yourself. Circle 3 (*I agree.*) OR
2 (*I'm not sure.*) OR 1 (*I can't do this.*).

I can give reasons using **because** and **because of**: **Because** the ceiling is high, I can't reach the smoke alarm. I can't reach the smoke alarm **because of** the high ceiling.	3 2 1
I can use **enough** and **too**: He **isn't tall enough** to reach the ceiling. The ceiling is **too high**.	3 2 1
I can identify facts and details in a reading.	3 2 1
I can write a letter of complaint.	3 2 1
I can read and understand an ad on a Web site.	3 2 1

C What's next? Choose one.

☐ I am ready for the unit test.   ☐ I need more practice with _____ .

Unit 4 Health

A Vocabulary Write eight new words you have learned.

_____ _____ _____ _____

_____ _____ _____ _____

B Skills and functions Read the sentences. Rate yourself. Circle 3 (*I agree.*) OR
2 (*I'm not sure.*) OR 1 (*I can't do this.*).

I can ask and answer questions using the present perfect with **lately** and **recently**: **Have** you **gained** weight **lately**? I **have lost** weight **recently**.	3 2 1
I can ask and answer questions with **used to**: **Did** you **use to** exercise? I **used to** exercise a lot.	3 2 1
I can identify the introduction and conclusion in a reading.	3 2 1
I can write a paragraph describing a healthful plant.	3 2 1
I can read and understand a medical history form.	3 2 1

C What's next? Choose one.

☐ I am ready for the unit test.   ☐ I need more practice with _____ .

Unit 5 Around town

A Vocabulary Write eight new words you have learned.

_____   _____   _____   _____

_____   _____   _____   _____

B Skills and functions Read the sentences. Rate yourself. Circle 3 (*I agree.*) OR 2 (*I'm not sure.*) OR 1 (*I can't do this.*).

I can ask and answer questions using verbs + infinitives: *Where do you plan **to go**? I plan **to go** to the park.*	3 2 1
I can ask and answer questions using the present perfect with ***already*** and ***yet***: *I **have already bought** tickets. **Have** you **bought** them **yet**?*	3 2 1
I can guess if a word has a positive or negative meaning.	3 2 1
I can write an e-mail about an event.	3 2 1
I can read and understand announcements about community events.	3 2 1

C What's next? Choose one.

☐ I am ready for the unit test.   ☐ I need more practice with _____ .

Unit 6 Time

A Vocabulary Write eight new words you have learned.

_____   _____   _____   _____

_____   _____   _____   _____

B Skills and functions Read the sentences. Rate yourself. Circle 3 (*I agree.*) OR 2 (*I'm not sure.*) OR 1 (*I can't do this.*).

I can use clauses with ***when***: ***When** she **feels** tired, she **takes** a break.*	3 2 1
I can use clauses with ***before*** and ***after***: ***Before** she **eats**, she **reads**. She **eats after** she **reads**.*	3 2 1
I can identify a definition, an explanation, or an example in a reading.	3 2 1
I can write a paragraph about a good or a weak time manager.	3 2 1
I can read and understand a pie chart.	3 2 1

C What's next? Choose one.

☐ I am ready for the unit test.   ☐ I need more practice with _____ .

Unit 7 Shopping

A Vocabulary Write eight new words you have learned.

_____   _____   _____   _____

_____   _____   _____   _____

B Skills and functions Read the sentences. Rate yourself. Circle 3 (*I agree.*) OR
2 (*I'm not sure.*) OR 1 (*I can't do this.*).

I can make suggestions using **could** and give advice using **should**: *You **could** get a smaller car. You **should** open a savings account.*	3 2 1
I can use gerunds after prepositions: *I'm thinking **about buying** a car.*	3 2 1
I can identify problems and solutions in a reading.	3 2 1
I can write a letter of advice.	3 2 1
I can read and understand a chart comparing checking accounts.	3 2 1

C What's next? Choose one.

☐ I am ready for the unit test.   ☐ I need more practice with _____ .

Unit 8 Work

A Vocabulary Write eight new words you have learned.

_____   _____   _____   _____

_____   _____   _____   _____

B Skills and functions Read the sentences. Rate yourself. Circle 3 (*I agree.*) OR
2 (*I'm not sure.*) OR 1 (*I can't do this.*).

I can ask and answer questions using the present perfect continuous: *How long **have** you **been living** here? I **have been living** here for a long time.*	3 2 1
I can use separable phrasal verbs: *He **handed out** the papers. He **handed** them **out**.*	3 2 1
I can scan a reading for specific information.	3 2 1
I can write a thank-you letter.	3 2 1
I can read and understand a chart with numbers comparing job growth.	3 2 1

C What's next? Choose one.

☐ I am ready for the unit test.   ☐ I need more practice with _____ .

Unit 9 Daily living

A Vocabulary Write eight new words you have learned.

_____   _____   _____   _____

_____   _____   _____   _____

B Skills and functions Read the sentences. Rate yourself. Circle 3 (*I agree.*) OR
2 (*I'm not sure.*) OR 1 (*I can't do this.*).

I can ask and answer questions using the past continuous: *What **were** you **doing** yesterday morning? I **was watching** TV.*	3 2 1
I can use **while** with the past continuous and **when** with the simple past: **While** I **was sleeping**, the fire **started. When** the fire **started**, I **was sleeping**.	3 2 1
I can identify time phrases in a reading.	3 2 1
I can write about an emergency.	3 2 1
I can read and understand a chart ranking safe states.	3 2 1

C What's next? Choose one.

☐ I am ready for the unit test.   ☐ I need more practice with _____ .

Unit 10 Leisure

A Vocabulary Write eight new words you have learned.

_____   _____   _____   _____

_____   _____   _____   _____

B Skills and functions Read the sentences. Rate yourself. Circle 3 (*I agree.*) OR
2 (*I'm not sure.*) OR 1 (*I can't do this.*).

I can use clauses with *if*: *I **will fly if** the fare **is** cheap.*	3 2 1
I can use clauses with **before** and **after** with future meaning: *He**'ll finish** school **before** he **takes** a vacation.*	3 2 1
I can find the explanation of words in a reading.	3 2 1
I can write about a tourist attraction.	3 2 1
I can read and understand information about hotels.	3 2 1

C What's next? Choose one.

☐ I am ready for the unit test.   ☐ I need more practice with _____ .

Verbs + gerunds

A gerund is the base form of a verb + *-ing*.
Gerunds often follow verbs that talk about preferences. Use a gerund like a noun.

Spelling rules for gerunds

*   Verbs ending in a vowel-consonant pair repeat the consonant before adding *-ing*:
    stop → stopping   get → getting
*   Verbs ending in silent *-e* drop the e before *-ing*:
    dance → dancing   exercise → exercising
    but:
    be → being   see → seeing

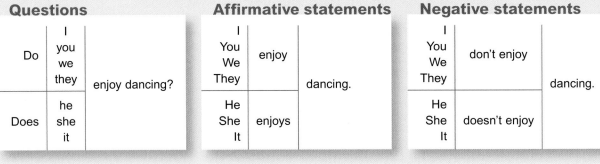

Questions		
Do	I you we they	enjoy dancing?
Does	he she it	

Affirmative statements		
I You We They	enjoy	dancing.
He She It	enjoys	

Negative statements		
I You We They	don't enjoy	dancing.
He She It	doesn't enjoy	

Verbs often followed by gerunds (verb + *-ing*)

avoid	feel like	love	quit
can't help	finish	mind	recommend
dislike	hate	miss	regret
enjoy	like	practice	suggest

Gerunds after prepositions

Prepositions are words like *in*, *of*, *about*, and *for*. Prepositions are often used in phrases with adjectives (*excited about*, *interested in*) and verbs (*think about*). Gerunds often follow these phrases.

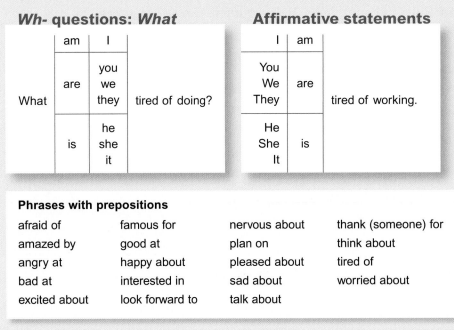

Wh- questions: *What*

What	am	I	tired of doing?
	are	you we they	
	is	he she it	

Affirmative statements

I	am	tired of working.
You We They	are	
He She It	is	

Phrases with prepositions

afraid of	famous for	nervous about	thank (someone) for
amazed by	good at	plan on	think about
angry at	happy about	pleased about	tired of
bad at	interested in	sad about	worried about
excited about	look forward to	talk about	

Verbs + infinitives

An infinitive is *to* + the base form of a verb.
Infinitives often follow certain verbs. See below for a list of verbs
that infinitives often follow.

Wh- questions: *Where*

Where	do	I you we they	want to go?
	does	he she it	

Affirmative statements

I You We They	want to go	to the park.
He She It	wants to go	

Yes / No questions

Do	I you we they	want to go?
Does	he she it	

Short answers

Yes,	I you we they	do.
	he she it	does.

No,	I you we they	don't.
	he she it	doesn't.

don't = do not
doesn't = does not

Verbs often followed by infinitives

agree	hope	need	promise
can / can't afford	intend	offer	refuse
decide	learn	plan	volunteer
expect	manage	prepare	want
help	mean	pretend	would like

Present perfect

The present perfect is *have* or *has* + past participle.
Use the present perfect to talk about actions that started in the past and continue to now.
See page 151 for a list of past participles with irregular verbs.

Use *how long* + present perfect to ask about the length of time.
Use *for* with a period of time to answer questions with *how long*.
Use *since* with a point in time to answer questions with *how long*.

Wh- questions: *How long*

How long	have	I you we they	been	here?
	has	he she it	been	

Affirmative statements: *for* and *since*

I You We They	have been	here	for two hours. since 6:00 p.m.
He She It	has been		

Use *ever* with the present perfect to ask *Yes / No* questions about things that happened at any time before now.

Yes / No questions: *ever*

Have	I you we they	ever	been late?
Has	he she it	ever	been late?

Short answers

Yes,	I you we they	have.	No,	I you we they	haven't.
Yes,	he she it	has.	No,	he she it	hasn't.

haven't = have not
hasn't = has not

Use *recently* and *lately* with the present perfect to talk about things that happened in the very recent past, not very long ago.

Yes / No questions: *recently* and *lately*

Have	I you we they	gone	to the movies recently? to the movies lately?
Has	he she it		

Present perfect continuous

The present perfect continuous is *have* or *has* + *been* + present participle.
Use the present perfect continuous to talk about actions that started in the past,
continue to now, and will probably continue in the future.

Yes / No questions

Have	I you we they	been working for a long time?
Has	he she it	

Short answers

Yes,	I you we they	have.		No,	I you we they	haven't.
	he she it	has.			he she it	hasn't.

Wh- questions: *How long*

How long	have	I you we they	been working?
	has	he she it	

Affirmative statements: *for* and *since*

I You We They	have been working	for a month. since October.
He She It	has been working	

used to

Used to talks about things that happened in the past.
Use *used to* to talk about a past situation or past habit that is not true now.

Yes / No questions

Did	I you he she it we you they	use to eat a lot?

Short answers

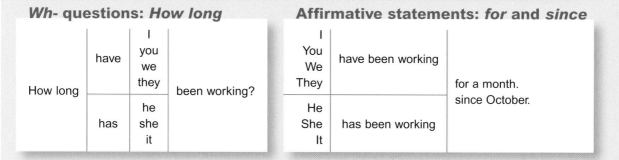

Yes,	I you he she it we you they	did.		No,	I you he she it we you they	didn't.

didn't = did not

Affirmative statements

I You He She It We You They	used to eat a lot.

Past continuous

Use the past continuous to talk about actions that were happening at a specific time in the past. The actions were not completed at that time.

Wh- questions: What

What	was	I	doing?
	were	you we they	
	was	he she it	

Affirmative statements

I	was	working.
You We They	were	
He She It	was	

Yes / No questions

Was	I	working?
Were	you we they	
Was	he she it	

Short answers

Yes,	I	was.
	you we they	were.
	he she it	was.

No,	I	wasn't.
	you we they	weren't.
	he she it	wasn't.

wasn't = was not
weren't = were not

could and should

Wh- questions: What

What	could should	I you he she it we you they	do?

Affirmative statements

I You He She It We You They	could should	work.

Negative statements

I You He She It We You They	couldn't shouldn't	work.

couldn't = could not
shouldn't = should not

Irregular verbs

Base form	Simple past	Past participle	Base form	Simple past	Past participle
be	was / were	been	leave	left	left
become	became	become	lose	lost	lost
begin	began	begun	make	made	made
break	broke	broken	meet	met	met
bring	brought	brought	pay	paid	paid
build	built	built	put	put	put
buy	bought	bought	read	read	read
catch	caught	caught	ride	rode	ridden
choose	chose	chosen	run	ran	run
come	came	come	say	said	said
cost	cost	cost	see	saw	seen
cut	cut	cut	sell	sold	sold
do	did	done	send	sent	sent
drink	drank	drunk	set	set	set
drive	drove	driven	show	showed	shown
eat	ate	eaten	sing	sang	sung
fall	fell	fallen	sit	sat	sat
feel	felt	felt	sleep	slept	slept
fight	fought	fought	speak	spoke	spoken
find	found	found	spend	spent	spent
fly	flew	flown	stand	stood	stood
forget	forgot	forgotten	steal	stole	stolen
get	got	gotten / got	swim	swam	swum
give	gave	given	take	took	taken
go	went	gone	teach	taught	taught
have	had	had	tell	told	told
hear	heard	heard	think	thought	thought
hide	hid	hidden	throw	threw	thrown
hit	hit	hit	understand	understood	understood
hold	held	held	wake	woke	woken
hurt	hurt	hurt	wear	wore	worn
keep	kept	kept	win	won	won
know	knew	known	write	wrote	written

Spelling rules for regular past participles

- To form the past participle of regular verbs, add -ed to the base form:
  listen → *listened*
- For regular verbs ending in a consonant + -y, change y to i and add -ed:
  study → *studied*
- For regular verbs ending in a vowel + -y, add -ed:
  play → *played*
- For regular verbs ending in -e, add -d:
  live → *lived*

Grammar explanations

Separable phrasal verbs

A phrasal verb is a verb + preposition. The meaning of the phrasal verb is different from the meaning of the verb alone.

> He *handed out* the papers to the class. = He *gave* the papers to the class.

A separable phrasal verb can have a noun between the verb and the preposition.

> He *handed **the papers** out.*

A separable phrasal verb can have a pronoun between the verb and the preposition.

> He *handed **them** out.*

Separable phrasal verbs

call back	cut off	find out	look up	throw away / out
call up	do over	give back	pick out	turn down
clean up	fill in	hand in	put away / back	turn off
cross out	fill out	hand out	shut off	turn up
cut down	fill up	leave on	tear up	

Comparisons

Use *more than*, *less than*, and *as much as* to compare nouns. A gerund is often used as a noun. You can compare activities by using gerunds and *more than*, *less than*, and *as much as*.

> I enjoy *walking more than driving.*
> She likes *cooking less than eating.*
> They enjoy *singing as much as dancing.*

Giving reasons and explanations with *because* and *because of*

Use a *because* clause to give explanations.

A *because* clause is the part of the sentence that begins with *because* + subject + verb or *because of* + noun phrase. Use a comma (,) when the *because* clause begins the sentence.

> I came to Ohio *because of my children.*
> *Because of my children,* I came to Ohio.

> I came to Ohio *because my children are here.*
> *Because my children are here,* I came to Ohio.

Adjectives with *enough* and *too*

Use an adjective + *enough* to talk about the right amount of something.

> The ladder is *tall enough* to reach the ceiling.

Use *not* + adjective + *enough* to talk about less than the right amount.

> The ladder is *not tall enough.*

Use *too* + adjective to talk about more than the right amount.

> The ladder is *too tall.*

Dependent clauses

A clause is a part of a sentence that has a subject and a verb. A dependent clause often begins with time words such as *when*, *before*, and *after*. The dependent clause can come at the beginning or end of a sentence. Use a comma (,) after dependent clauses that come at the beginning of a sentence. Do not use a comma when a dependent clause comes at the end of a sentence.

when: Use *when* + present time verbs to talk about habits.

> *When I have a lot to do,* I make a to-do list.
> I make a to-do list *when I have a lot to do.*

after: Use *after* to order events in a sentence. *After* introduces the first event. Use *after* with the simple present to talk about habits.

> First, I eat dinner. Second, I watch the news. =
> I watch the news *after I eat dinner.*
> *After I eat dinner,* I watch the news.

Use *after* with the simple present and future to talk about future plans.

> First, he'll finish school. Second, he'll take a vacation. =
> He'll take a vacation *after he finishes school.*
> *After he finishes school,* he'll take a vacation.

before: Use *before* to order events in a sentence. *Before* introduces the second event. Use *before* with the simple present to talk about habits.

> First, she reads the newspaper. Second, she eats breakfast. =
> She reads the newspaper *before she eats breakfast.*
> *Before she eats breakfast,* she reads the newspaper.

Use *before* with the simple present and future to talk about future plans.

> First, he'll finish school. Second, he'll take a vacation. =
> He'll finish school *before he takes a vacation.*
> *Before he takes a vacation,* he'll finish school.

when and ***while***: Use *when* or *while* with the past continuous and simple past to show that one past action interrupted another past action.
Use *when* with the simple past for the action that interrupted.

> They were sleeping *when the fire started.*
> *When the fire started,* they were sleeping.

Use *while* with the past continuous to show the action that was happening before the interruption.

> The fire started *while they were sleeping.*
> *While they were sleeping,* the fire started.

if: Use *if* clauses to talk about future possibility. Use the simple present in the clause with *if*. Use the future in the other clause to talk about what could happen.

> She won't go *if the weather is bad.*
> *If the weather is bad,* she won't go.

Self-study audio script

Welcome

Page 3, Exercise 2A – Track 2

1. **A** Where are you from?
   B I'm from Taipei, Taiwan.
2. **A** What did you do there?
   B I was a housewife.
3. **A** When did you move here?
   B I moved here in March 2006.
4. **A** Where do you live?
   B I live in Monterey Park.
5. **A** How long does it take you to get to school?
   B It takes me about 30 minutes to get to school.
6. **A** Are you married?
   B Yes, I'm married.
7. **A** What will you do next year?
   B I'll look for a job.

Page 4, Exercise 3A – Track 3

1. Diego Mata moved to the United States in 2005.
2. He got a job at a gas station. He pumped gas and helped customers.
3. From 2005 to 2007, he took classes in English and auto mechanics.
4. Now Diego works as an auto mechanic. He fixes cars every day.
5. Diego is taking a citizenship class right now.
6. He will become a U.S. citizen next year.

Page 4, Exercise 3B – Track 4

Oksana Petrova was born in Russia. She had a very good job there. She was a teacher.

In 2005, Oksana left Russia and moved to the United States. In 2006, she started a job as a teacher's assistant, and she is still working there now. She usually works five days a week.

Oksana wants to become a teacher in the U.S. She is studying English at night now. Next year, she will go to a university. With hard work and good luck, Oksana will graduate in four years.

Page 5, Exercise 4A – Track 5

Silvia's Goal

Silvia wants to open her own beauty salon someday. To reach her goal, she needs to take three steps. First, she needs to go to beauty school for two years. Second, she needs to take an exam to get her license. Third, she needs to work in a salon to get experience. Silvia hopes to become a business owner in five years. She doesn't want to work for anyone else.

Unit 1: Personal information

Lesson A: Get ready

Page 7, Exercises 2A and 2B – Track 6

A Hey, Danny, I am *so* tired this morning. I need a break. Let's get a cup of coffee.

B You're always tired on Mondays, Fernando. So, how was your weekend? Wild, as usual?

A Yeah, I guess. You know I like dancing, right? Well, last night, my girlfriend and I went to that new Cuban dance club – Club Havana.

B Oh, the one on, uh, Fourteenth Street?

A Yeah. Fourteenth Street. The place was full of people, and the music was incredible. We danced until, oh, it was about 1:30 in the morning. . . . Hey, you know what? You should come with us next time.

B Me? No. Oh, no. I don't like dancing.

A You're kidding. You don't like dancing? You really don't like *dancing*?

B Yeah, well, you know, Fernando, you're really outgoing and friendly, but I'm not outgoing. I'm not a party animal like you. I'm kind of shy. When I was a kid, I disliked going to parties, and I never learned how to dance.

A Really? That's too bad. But then, what *do* you enjoy doing?

B OK. This weekend, for example, I had a really nice, *quiet* weekend. I worked on my car, I watched some TV, I studied for my business class, and . . .

A Wow, Danny! You mean you were home the whole time? You didn't go anywhere?

B Nope. I was home alone the whole weekend. Well, I went to the auto-parts store. See, I like staying home more than going out. But I'd like to find a girlfriend who likes staying home, too.

A A girlfriend? How are you going to find a girlfriend if you stay home all the time?

B Good question. Come on. Let's get back to work.

Page 7, Exercise 2C – Track 7

Fernando and Danny are talking about their weekend. Fernando is a very friendly and outgoing person. He enjoys dancing. Last night, he went to a dance club and stayed until 1:30 in the morning. Danny thinks Fernando is a party animal.

Danny is different from Fernando. He is shy and quiet. He dislikes dancing. Danny was home alone the whole weekend. He likes staying at home more than going out. He wants a girlfriend who likes staying home, too.

Lesson D: Reading

Page 12, Exercise 2 – Track 8

Your Personality and Your Job

What is the perfect job for you? It depends a lot on your personality. People think, act, and feel in different ways, and there are interesting jobs for every kind of person. Three common personality types are outgoing, intellectual, and creative.

Outgoing people enjoy meeting others and helping them. They are good talkers. They are friendly, and they get along well with other people. They often become nurses, counselors, teachers, or social workers.

Intellectual people like thinking about problems and finding answers to hard questions. They often enjoy reading and playing games like chess. Many intellectual people like working alone more than working in a group. They may become scientists, computer programmers, or writers.

Creative people enjoy making things. They like to imagine things that are new and different. Many of them become artists such as painters, dancers, or musicians. Architects, designers, and photographers are other examples of creative jobs.

Before you choose a career, think about your personality type. If you want to be happy in your work, choose the right job for your personality.

Unit 2: At school

Lesson A: Get ready

Page 19, Exercises 2A and 2B – Track 9

A Hi, Alex.

B Hi, Bella.

A How long have you been in the library?

B For about two hours.

A How's it going?

B Um, not great.

A Why? What's the matter?

B I'm so discouraged. Look at this mess! I have to finish reading this book. Then I have to write a paper and study for a test. Where do I start!

A Well, Alex, have you ever tried making a to-do list?

B A to-do list?

A Yeah. You make a list of all the things you have to do. Then you do the most important things first.

B A to-do list. No, I've never tried that. I usually try to do six things at the same time. Let's see. Right now, the most important thing is to finish

reading this book. But it's so boring. I can't concentrate.

A You need to be more active, Alex. Don't just read the book. You know, underline important ideas, write notes, repeat the main ideas to yourself. Those things will help you concentrate.

B Hmm. I think I can do that. But there's another problem.

A What's that?

B Too many new words! I can't remember all of them.

A Hmm. Well, here's an idea. Write important words on index cards. Take the cards with you, and study them everywhere – on the bus, during your break at work, and before you go to bed. . . .

B OK, OK! I get it: Study smarter – not harder. Thanks, Bella.

Page 19, Exercise 2C – Track 10

Alex has been at the library for more than two hours, and he is very discouraged. He has many things to do. He needs to study for a test and write a paper. He needs to finish reading a book, but he can't concentrate. He says the book is boring.

Alex's friend Bella gives him some study advice. First, she tells Alex to make a list of all the things he needs to do. Next, she says he has to be a more active reader. For example, he should underline main ideas in his textbooks. Finally, she tells him to write vocabulary words on index cards and study them when he has free time.

With Bella's help, Alex plans to study smarter, not harder.

Lesson D: Reading

Page 24, Exercise 2 – Track 11

Strategies for Learning English

Have you ever felt discouraged because it's hard to speak and understand English? Don't give up! Here are three strategies to help you learn faster and remember more.

Strategy Number 1 – Set goals.

Have you ever set goals for

learning English? When you set goals, you decide what you want to learn. Then you make a plan to help you reach your goals. Maybe your goal is to learn more vocabulary. There are many ways to do this. For example, you can read in English for 15 minutes every day. You can also learn one new word every day.

Strategy Number 2 – Look for opportunities to practice English.

Talk to everyone. Speak with people in the store, at work, and in the park. Don't worry about making mistakes. And don't forget to ask questions. For example, if your teacher uses a word you don't understand, ask a question like "What does that word mean?"

Strategy Number 3 – Guess.

Don't try to translate every word. When you read, concentrate on clues such as pictures or other words in the sentence to help you understand. You can also make guesses when you are talking to people. For example, look at their faces and hand gestures – the way they move their hands – to help you guess the meaning.

Set goals, look for opportunities to practice, and guess. Do these things every day, and you will learn more English!

Unit 3: Friends and family

Lesson A: Get ready

Page 33, Exercises 2A and 2B – Track 12

A Hello?

B Maria? Hi. It's Ana.

A Hey. Hi, Ana. How are you?

B Good, thanks. But I've been super busy. . . . Listen, Maria, do you have a minute to talk? Are you eating dinner?

A No, we've eaten. What's up?

B Well, I need a favor.

A Sure, Ana, what is it?

B The smoke alarm in my kitchen is beeping. *Beep, beep, beep!* I need to change the battery, but the ceiling's too high. Can I borrow your ladder?

A Sure, but I have a better idea. Um, Daniel can come over and change the battery for you.

B Really? Are you sure he has enough time?

A Oh, Ana, you know Daniel. He is never too busy to help a neighbor. He'll come over in five minutes.

B Thanks. I really appreciate it. I owe you one. See you. . . .

A Wait, Ana, I want to ask you something. Did you hear our noisy neighbors last Saturday night? They had a party until three in the morning. Because of the noise, we couldn't sleep at all.

B Gosh, that's too bad, Maria. I didn't hear anything. But you should complain to the manager.

A Yeah, I know. I'll do it tomorrow.

Page 33, Exercise 2C – Track 13

Ana and Maria are neighbors. Ana calls Maria because she needs a favor. The smoke alarm in Ana's kitchen is beeping. She needs to change the battery, but the ceiling in her kitchen is too high. Ana asks to borrow Maria's ladder.

Maria says her husband, Daniel, will come over with a ladder and help Ana. Ana says, "I owe you one." This means she appreciates Maria and Daniel's help, and she will do a favor for them in the future.

Next, Maria tells Ana about their noisy neighbors. The neighbors had a party on Saturday night. Because of the noise, Maria and Daniel couldn't sleep. Ana tells Maria that she should complain to the apartment manager.

Lesson D: Reading

Page 38, Exercise 2 – Track 14

Neighborhood Watch Success Story
by Latisha Holmes, President, Rolling Hills Neighborhood Watch
  People often ask me about the role of Neighborhood Watch. My answer is: Because of Neighborhood Watch, our neighborhood is safer and nicer. Members of Neighborhood Watch help each other and watch out for each other. For example, we watch out for our neighbors' houses when they aren't home. We help elderly neighbors with yard work. Once a month, we get together to paint over graffiti.

  Last Wednesday, the Neighborhood Watch team had another success story. Around 8:30 p.m., members of our Neighborhood Watch were out on a walk. Near the Corner Café, they noticed two men next to George Garcia's car. George lives at 1157 Rolling Hills Drive. The men were trying to break into the car. Suddenly, the car alarm went off. The men ran away and got into a car down the street. But they weren't quick enough. Our Neighborhood Watch members wrote down the car's license plate number and called the police. Later that night, the police arrested the two men.

  I would like to congratulate our Neighborhood Watch team on their good work. Because of their good work, Rolling Hills is a safer neighborhood today.

  For information about Neighborhood Watch, please call 213-555-1234.

Unit 4: Health

Lesson A: Get ready

Page 45, Exercises 2A and 2B – Track 15

A Hello, Stanley. I haven't seen you for some time. How've you been?

B Busy. I've been working really hard.

A I see. So what brings you here today?

B Well, you know, I've always been healthy, but, uh, I've been really tired lately.

A Uh-huh. Well, let's take a look at your chart. . . . Ah, I see you've gained 20 pounds since last year.

B Yeah. I used to exercise a lot, but now I just work. Work, eat, and sleep.

A Well, you know, gaining weight can make you feel tired, Stanley. You need to start exercising again. Can you try walking for 30 minutes each day?

B I don't have time. I'm working a lot these days – sometimes 10, even 12 hours a day.

A Hmm. Well, then, can you walk or ride a bicycle to work? And at work, don't use the elevator. Take the stairs.

B Well, I guess, I can try.

A Good. Now, let's see. You also have high blood pressure. Tell me about your diet. What have you eaten since yesterday?

B Well, last night I had a hamburger with fries and a soft drink.

A Fat, salt, and sugar! They're all bad for your blood pressure, Stanley. What about today?

B I haven't eaten anything today.

A No breakfast? Well, of course you feel tired! You need to change your diet, Stanley. Eat more fish and more vegetables. Give up fast food. No hamburgers! No fries! They're really bad for your health.

B That's really hard. I'm so busy right now. I don't have time to . . .

A Listen, Stanley. You're 40 years old. Do you want to have a heart attack? This is my advice. You need to make real changes, or you'll need to start taking pills and all kinds of medication.

B OK. I'll try.

Page 45, Exercise 2C – Track 16

Stanley is at the doctor's office. His health has always been good, but he has been really tired lately. The doctor looks at Stanley's chart. He sees a couple of problems. One problem is Stanley's weight. He has gained 20 pounds. Another problem is his blood pressure. The doctor tells him he needs regular exercise – for example, walking or riding a bike. He also tells

Stanley to change his diet – to eat more fish and vegetables. If Stanley doesn't do these things, he will need to take pills and other medication. Stanley wants to be healthy, so he is going to try to follow the doctor's advice.

Lesson D: Reading

Page 50, Exercise 2 – Track 17

Two Healthful Plants

Since the beginning of history, people in every culture have used plants to stay healthy and to prevent sickness. Garlic and chamomile are two healthful plants.

Garlic is a plant in the onion family. The green stem and the leaves of the garlic plant grow above the ground. The root – the part under the ground – is a bulb with sections called cloves. They look like the pieces of an orange. The bulb is the part that people have traditionally used for medicine. They have used it for insect bites, cuts, earaches, and coughs. Today, some people also use it to treat high blood pressure and high cholesterol.

Chamomile is a small, pretty plant with flowers that bloom from late summer to early fall. The flowers have white petals and a yellow center. Many people use dried chamomile flowers to make tea. Some people give the tea to babies with upset stomachs. They also drink chamomile tea to feel better when they have a cold or the flu, poor digestion, or trouble falling asleep.

For thousands of years, people everywhere have grown garlic, chamomile, and other herbal medicines in their gardens. Today, you can buy them in health-food stores. You can get them in dried, powdered, or pill form.

Unit 5: Around town

Lesson A: Get ready

Page 59, Exercises 2A and 2B – Track 18

A Mei, I'm so glad tomorrow is Friday. It's been a long week.

B That's for sure. Hmm. What would you like to do this weekend, Wen?

A Well, there are a few movies we haven't seen yet, or we could go to a concert downtown.

B Oh, we can't afford to go to concerts, Wen. They're too expensive. And I'm sort of tired of going to the movies.

A OK, so let's do something different on Sunday, something we haven't done yet this summer.

B Like what? Got any ideas?

A Let's check the newspaper for community events. Maybe we'll find something free right here in the neighborhood. Let's take a look. . . . Hmm. We have a lot of options. Here's something interesting. There's a concert in the park on Sunday at noon, admission is free.

B And here, look, there's a free walking tour of the gardens on Sunday at eleven o'clock.

A Here's another option, Mei. The Museum of Art is free the first Sunday of every month. There's an exhibit of modern art showing now. The museum opens at ten a.m.

B Oh. And here's something at the library: free storytelling for children on Sunday at ten-thirty. Everything is happening on the same day at the same time! What do you want to do, Wen?

A Why don't we go to the library first? Then, let's plan to go to the concert if the weather is nice. And then maybe later, we can go to the art museum.

B Yeah. That sounds good. I'll check the weather forecast for the weekend. Then we can decide.

Page 59, Exercise 2C – Track 19

It is Thursday. Wen and Mei are talking about their plans for the weekend. They can't afford to spend a lot of money on entertainment. They decide to check the newspaper for free community events on Sunday. They have many options. There's an outdoor concert in the park, a walking tour of the gardens, a modern art exhibit at the art museum, and storytelling for children at the library. All these events have free admission.

The problem is that all these things are happening on Sunday at the same time. Mei and Wen decide to take their son to storytelling first. Then, if the weather is nice, they will go to the concert. Later, they might go to the art museum.

Lesson D: Reading

Page 64, Exercise 2 – Track 20

Salsa Starz at Century Park

If you missed the outdoor concert at Century Park last Saturday evening, you missed a great night of salsa music and dancing – and the admission was free!

The performers were the popular band Salsa Starz. Bandleader Ernesto Sanchez led the five-piece group and two dancers. Sanchez is a versatile musician. He sang and played maracas and guitar. The other musicians were also superb. The group's excellent playing and great energy galvanized the crowd. No one sat down during the entire show!

However, the evening had some problems. At first, the sound level of the music was excessive. I had to wear earplugs. Then, the level was too low. The change in sound was irritating. In addition, the stage was plain and unremarkable. I expected to see lights and lots of color at the performance. The weather was another problem. The night started out clear. By ten p.m., some ominous black clouds moved in, and soon it started to rain. The band intended to play until eleven, but the show ended early because of the rain.

Century Park has free concerts every Saturday evening in July and August. If you haven't attended one of these concerts yet, plan to go next weekend. But take an umbrella!

Unit 6: Time

Lesson A: Get ready

Page 71, Exercises 2A and 2B – Track 21

A Winston, what are you doing?

B I'm thinking.

A No, you're not. You're procrastinating. You always procrastinate. I'm getting very impatient with you! I asked you to take out the trash two hours ago, and you haven't done it yet.

B Aw, Mom.

A Do you have homework?

B Yeah, but . . . I can't decide what to do first.

A Hmm. Would you like some help?

B Well, uh, yeah, I guess.

A OK. So, why don't you make a to-do list. You know, write down all the tasks you have to do.

B OK. I've got . . . math, an English essay, and a history project.

A Uh-huh. What else?

B I have to practice guitar. I have a lesson tomorrow.

A And don't forget the trash. Write that down, too.

B OK. Now what?

A Prioritize. What are you going to do first, second, third, and so on?

B Well, guitar is first. It's the most fun.

A Nuh-uh. I don't think so. Homework and chores are first. Guitar is last.

B OK. Should I start with math, English, or history?

A Hmm. When are they due?

B Math and English are due tomorrow.

A And the history project?

B The deadline is next week. On Tuesday.

A OK. So do math and English tonight. You can do the history project over the weekend.

B OK, math and English tonight. Which one should I do first?

A Well, I always do the hardest thing first.

B English is a lot harder than math.

A OK. So English, then math, then guitar. But before you do anything, . . .

B Yeah, I know. Take out the trash.

A Right.

Page 71, Exercise 2C – Track 22

Winston is listening to music in his room. His mother comes in and tells him to stop procrastinating. She is very impatient because he isn't taking out the trash and he isn't doing his homework.

Winston has too many things to do. His mother suggests making a to-do list. First, she tells him to list all the tasks he needs to do. Next, she tells him to prioritize – to put his tasks in order of importance. Winston wants to practice guitar first because it's the most fun. His mother says he needs to do his homework and chores first. He decides to do his English and math homework first because they are due the next day. He also has a history project, but the deadline is next Tuesday. After he finishes his homework, he will practice guitar. But before he does anything else, he has to take out the trash.

Lesson D: Reading

Page 76, Exercise 2 – Track 23

Rules About Time

Every culture has rules about time. These rules are usually unspoken, but everybody knows them.

In some countries such as the United States, England, and Canada, punctuality is an unspoken rule. It is important to be on time, especially in business. People usually arrive a little early for business appointments. Business meetings often have strict beginning and ending times. When you are late, other people might think you are rude, disorganized, or irresponsible.

These countries also have cultural rules about time in social situations. For example, when an invitation for dinner says six p.m., it is impolite to arrive more than five or ten minutes late. On the other hand, when the invitation is for a cocktail party from six to eight or a reception from three-thirty to five-thirty, you can arrive anytime between those hours. For public events with specific starting times – movies, concerts, plays – you should arrive a few minutes before the event begins. In fact, some theaters do not allow people to enter if they arrive after the event has started.

Other cultures have different rules about time. In Brazil, it is not unusual for guests to arrive an hour or two after a social event begins. In the Philippines, it is not uncommon for people to miss scheduled events – a class or an appointment – to meet a friend at the airport. Many Filipinos believe that relationships with people are more important than keeping a schedule.

Unit 7: Shopping

Lesson A: Get ready

Page 85, Exercises 2A and 2B – Track 24

A Julie, look at this car! "Automatic transmission, air-conditioning, leather seats, sun roof, power windows, . . ." It's got everything, and it's only $27,500.

B Ken, are you crazy? With tax and fees, that's about $30,000! We can't afford $30,000 for a car! Where . . . where are we going to get the money? The balance in our savings account is less than $8,000!

A No problem. Look here. It says, "Special financing available. Only 4% interest with 60 months to pay off the loan!"

B Sixty months to pay! That's five years! We're going to pay for that car every month for five years. Ken, you know I'm afraid of getting into debt. We have bills to pay every month. And we need to save money for college for the kids.

A Well, Julie, tell me: *Do* we need a car, or *don't* we need a car? Our old one always needs repair, and it's . . .

B OK, OK. We *do* need a car. But we don't need a new car. We could look for a used car. Let's go across the street and look. I'm sure we can find a good used car for $10,000 or even less than that.

A Yeah, but, Julie, look at this car. It's a beauty! We should get it. We can buy the car on credit. Everybody does it!

B No, not everybody! My father always paid cash for everything. He didn't even have a credit card!

A Well, your father never had any fun. And . . . I'm *not* your father!

Page 85, Exercise 2C – Track 25

Ken and his wife, Julie, are looking at cars. Ken wants to buy a new car that costs over $27,000. Julie thinks that they can't afford to spend that much money. The balance in their savings account is less than $8,000. She's afraid of getting into debt. But Ken says they can get financing to help pay for the new car. The interest rate is low, and they can take five years to pay off the loan. Ken isn't worried about buying things on credit.

Julie disagrees. She suggests that they could buy a used car. She says her father never had a credit card. He always paid cash for everything.

Lesson D: Reading
Page 90, Exercise 2 – Track 26

A Credit Card Nightmare

Sun Hi and Joseph Kim got their first credit card a week after they got married. At first, they paid off the balance every month.

The couple's problems began after they bought a new house. They bought new furniture, a big-screen television, and two new computers. To pay for everything, they applied for more and more credit. Soon they had six different credit cards, and they were more than $18,000 in debt.

"It was a nightmare!" says Mrs. Kim. "The interest rates were 19 percent to 24 percent. Our minimum payments were over $750 a month. We both got second jobs, but it wasn't enough. I was so worried about paying off the debt, I cried all the time."

Luckily, the Kims found a solution. They met Dolores Delgado, a debt counselor. With her help, they looked at all of their living expenses and made a family budget. They combined their six credit card payments into one monthly payment with a lower interest rate. Now, their monthly budget for all living expenses is $3,400. Together they earn $3,900 a month. That leaves $500 for paying off their debt.

"We've cut up our credit cards," says Mr. Kim. "No more expensive furniture! In five years, we can pay off our debt. Now we know. Credit cards are dangerous!"

Unit 8: Work

Lesson A: Get ready
Page 97, Exercises 2A and 2B – Track 27

A Good morning, Tony. Thanks for coming in. I'm Ken Leong, personnel manager for the company.

B Nice to meet you, Mr. Leong.

A So, I have your resume right here, and I understand you're interested in the job of shipping-and-receiving clerk.

B Yes, that's right. I'm applying for the shipping-and-receiving clerk position.

A OK. I'd like to ask you a few questions.

B Sure, go ahead.

A Uh. First of all, could you tell me a little about your background? Where are you from? What kind of work have you done?

B Well, I was born in Peru and lived there for 18 years. I finished high school there, and then I came here with my family. I've been living here for two years.

A OK. And are you currently employed?

B Uh. Sorry?

A Are you working now?

B Yes, I've been working part-time as a teacher's assistant at an elementary school for about a year. And I'm also going to community college at night. I want to get a degree in accounting.

A Oh. That's good. What office machines can you use?

B Uh. I can use a computer, a fax machine, a scanner, and a copying machine.

A Excellent. Those skills will be useful in this job. You'll need to take inventory and order supplies. Now, Tony, can you tell me about some of your strengths?

B Um. Excuse me?

A Your strengths – you know, your personal qualities. What makes you a good person for this job?

B Well, I'm very responsible and reliable. If I have a deadline, I come in early or stay late to finish the job. Also, I get along with everyone. I never have problems working with people. I like everyone. And they like me.

A That's great. Can you work any shift?

B Well, I prefer the day shift because I have classes at night.

A OK, Tony. There's going to be an opening in the day shift soon. I'll get back to you next week sometime.

B Thank you, Mr. Leong. I appreciate that. It was nice to meet you.

A You, too. I'll give you a call.

Page 97, Exercise 2C – Track 28

Tony has been working as a teacher's assistant for about a year. He is also going to college part-time to get a degree in accounting. Right now, Tony is at a job interview with Mr. Leong, the personnel manager.

Mr. Leong asks about Tony's background. Tony says he is from Peru and has been living in the United States for two years. Next, Mr. Leong asks about Tony's work experience, and Tony says that now he is employed at an elementary school. Finally, Mr. Leong asks about Tony's personal strengths. Tony says he is responsible and reliable, and he gets along with everybody. Tony says he prefers to work the day shift. Mr. Leong says he will contact Tony next week.

Lesson D: Reading

Page 102, Exercise 2 – Track 29

Eden's Blog
Monday 9/15

Hello fellow job searchers! I have been looking for a job for several weeks. Everyone tells me that it's critical to network, so I've been telling everyone I know. I've been calling friends, relatives, and teachers to tell them about my job search. I hope I'll get a job interview!

Tuesday 9/16

Today, I went to a job fair at my college. I filled out several applications and handed out some resumes. There were about 20 different companies there. Several of them said they were going to call me back. Wish me luck!

Wednesday 9/24

I've been feeling depressed about the job search lately, but my counselor at school told me I shouldn't give up. He said I need to be patient. Today, I organized my papers. I made lists of the places I have applied to and the people I have talked to. I also did some more research online.

Thursday 9/25

Great news! One of the companies from the job fair finally called me back! I've been preparing for the job interview all day. I'm really excited. I'm going to have a practice interview with some classmates today. That will prepare me for the real one.

Monday 9/29

I had my interview today! I gave the interviewer a big smile and a firm handshake. I answered her questions with confidence. I'll let you know if I get the job. If you have any good job-searching tips, please share them with me!

Unit 9: Daily living

Lesson A: Get ready

Page 111, Exercises 2A and 2B – Track 30

A Hello?

B Samantha, this is Monica.

A Monica! I've been waiting for you to call. But, um, you sound really strange. Are you OK?

B Well, actually, no! I'm not. . . . Not at all. Somebody broke into our house tonight.

A Broke into your house? That's terrible! When? How?

B Well, around 7:30, we went over to the Morenos next door to watch a movie. And while we were there, someone broke into our house and robbed us. They stole our TV, DVD player, jewelry, and some cash. I still can't believe it.

A Ugh. That's awful. How did the robber get in?

B He broke a window in the back bedroom. You should see the mess – there's glass all over the floor, and there are books and CDs and clothes all over the place. And, Samantha, they took my mother's ring. I'm so upset.

A Oh, did you call the police?

B Of course. They've already been here.

A What's happening to our neighborhood? We never used to have so much crime. When the kids were little, we didn't even lock the front door!

B Well, I'm just glad we weren't home when it happened.

A Oh, Monica, I feel so bad for you. And I'm worried. Did you hear someone robbed Mr. Purdy last week, too, while he was out taking a walk? I think we should start a Neighborhood Watch program, don't you?

B Yeah, we've been talking about that for months. I agree, it's time we finally did it. But right now, I have to clean up this mess.

A Do you want me to come over, Monica? I could help you clean up.

B You're the best, Samantha. Yeah, come as quickly as you can. Thanks.

Page 111, Exercise 2C – Track 31

Monica calls her friend Samantha with bad news. While Monica and her husband were at a neighbor's house, someone broke into their home and stole their TV, DVD player, jewelry, and some cash. Monica is upset because the robber took her mother's ring. She says the person got in through a window in the back bedroom.

Samantha is worried. She says they never used to have so much crime in their neighborhood. She tells Monica that last week someone robbed their neighbor Mr. Purdy, too. Samantha thinks they should start a Neighborhood Watch program. Monica agrees, but first, she needs to clean up the mess in her house. Samantha offers to come over and help.

Lesson D: Reading

Page 116, Exercise 2 – Track 32

Home Is More Than a Building

A few months ago, Pedro Ramirez, 45, lost his job in a grocery store. To pay the bills, he got a part-time job at night. Several days later, Pedro's wife, Luisa, gave him a big surprise. She was pregnant with their sixth child. Pedro was happy but worried. "How am I going to support another child without a full-time job?" he wondered.

That evening, Pedro and Luisa got some more news. A fire was coming near their home. By the next morning, the fire was very close. The police ordered every family in the neighborhood to evacuate. The Ramirez family moved quickly. While Pedro was gathering their legal documents, Luisa grabbed the family photographs, and the children put their pets – a cat and a bird – in the family's truck. Then, the family drove to the home of their eldest daughter, one hour away.

About 24 hours later, Pedro and Luisa got very bad news. The fire destroyed their home. They lost almost everything. With no home, only part-time work, and a baby coming, Pedro was even more worried about the future.

For the next three months, the Ramirez family stayed with their daughter while workers were rebuilding their home. Many generous people helped them during that difficult time. Friends took them shopping for clothes. Strangers left gifts at their door. A group of children collected $500 to buy bicycles for the Ramirez children.

Because of all the help from friends and neighbors, the Ramirez family was able to rebuild their lives. Two months after the fire, Luisa mailed out holiday cards with this message: "Home is more than a building. Home is wherever there is love."

Unit 10: Leisure

Lesson A: Get ready

Page 123, Exercises 2A and 2B – Track 33

A I'm so exhausted! I really need a vacation.

B You know, my work is pretty slow right now. I can talk to my boss. Maybe he'll give me a few days off.

A Oh, Ricardo, what a great idea. We haven't had a family vacation in two years.

B Where would you like to go, Felicia?

A We could go to San Francisco. Michelle's six – she's old enough to enjoy it, don't you think?

B Well, let's see if there are any deals on any of the Internet travel sites. . . . Look, if we book a flight seven days ahead, we can get a round-trip ticket for $99.

A That's not too expensive. Are there any discounts for children?

B Hmm. Let's see. . . . I don't think so.

A Oh, that's too bad. What about hotel rates?

B Not cheap. Summer is the height of the tourist season. If we stay in a nice hotel, it's going to cost at least $150 a night.

A Plus the room tax, don't forget. You have to add on an extra 14% or something like that.

B Right. I forgot about that. So if the three of us take this trip, and if we stay in San Francisco just three days, it's going to cost almost $900.

A That's a lot to spend for just a three-day vacation, Ricardo. Maybe we should just go camping instead.

B Yeah, you're probably right. We could go to Big Bear Lake. If we do that, how much will it cost?

A Well, gas will probably cost about $50, the campsite will cost about $25 a night, and then there's food – but that won't be too much if we barbecue.

B Michelle will probably have more fun camping, too.

A I agree. So what do you think? Should we make a reservation?

B I'll reserve the campsite after I talk to my boss tomorrow.

A I hope he says yes. We really need a vacation.

Page 123, Exercise 2C – Track 34

Felicia is exhausted. She needs a vacation. Her husband, Ricardo, says maybe he can ask his boss for a few days off. Felicia says she would like to go to San Francisco. She and her husband look for special travel discounts on the Internet. If they book a flight at least seven days ahead, they can get a round-trip ticket for less than $100. On the other hand, hotel room rates will be high because summer is the most popular tourist season. Also, there is a room tax on hotel rooms in San Francisco. They figure out that a three-day trip to San Francisco will cost almost $900. Felicia and her husband decide to change their plans. If they go camping, they will save a lot of money and their daughter will have more fun. Felicia's husband will reserve the campsite after he talks to his boss.

Lesson D: Reading
Page 128, Exercise 2 – Track 35

The Rock: San Francisco's Biggest Tourist Attraction

Alcatraz, a small, rocky island in the middle of San Francisco Bay, was once the most famous prison in the United States. For a period of 29 years, from 1934 to 1963, over 1,500 dangerous criminals lived in the prison's 378 cells. People believed that it was impossible to escape from Alcatraz Island. However, in 1962 two brothers, John and Clarence Anglin, and another man named Frank Morris escaped on a raft made of raincoats. A famous movie, *Escape from Alcatraz*, tells this amazing story. Other famous prisoners who lived on the island included Al Capone, the gangster, and Robert Stroud, the "Birdman of Alcatraz."

Alcatraz prison closed in 1963. The island became a national park, and since then, it has been a major attraction for tourists from all over the world. These days, many people call Alcatraz by its popular name, "The Rock."

In the summer, it is wise to buy tickets to the island in advance because the ferries sell out. Evening tours are less crowded. The admission prices listed include the ferry, tickets, and an audio tour.

General admission:

Adult (18 to 61), $24.50

Junior (12 to 17), $24.50

Child (5 to 11), $15.25

Senior (62 or older), $23.25

Illustration credits

Ken Batelman: 87, 101

Cyrille Berger: 17, 35, 46, 69, 100, 125

Nina Edwards: 34, 63, 127

Travis Foster: 9, 36, 47, 81, 114

Chuck Gonzales: 10, 75, 89, 115

Brad Hamann: 37, 38, 49, 73, 99, 118

Ben Kirchner: 2, 6, 18, 32, 44, 58, 70, 84, 96, 110, 122

Monika Roe: 43, 48, 92, 113, 116

Photography credits

12 (*clockwise from top right*) ©Inmagine; ©Jupiter Images; ©L. Lefkowitz/Getty Images

14 (*clockwise from top left*) ©Inmagine; ©Inmagine; ©Jupiter Images; ©Inmagine; ©Inmagine; ©David Woolley/Getty Images

16 (*top to bottom*) ©Bernd Fuchs/Getty Images; ©Inmagine; ©Inmagine

50 (*both*) ©Inmagine

52 (*left to right*) ©Historical Picture Archive/Corbis; ©William Rhind/Fine Rare Prints; ©Dorling Kindersly/Punchstock

53 ©Inmagine

64 ©Chris Pizzello/Reuters/Corbis

90 (*left to right*) ©Inmagine; ©Jerry Arcieri/Corbis

92 ©Inmagine

102 ©Steve Prezant/Corbis

112 ©Inmagine

121 (*top to bottom*) ©Shutterstock; ©Shutterstock; ©Inmagine; ©Shutterstock; ©Jupiter Images; ©Inmagine

128 ©Jupiter Images

130 (*left to right*) ©San Diego County Fair; ©Jupiter Images; ©San Diego County Fair

133 (*clockwise from top left*) ©Jupiter Images; ©Inmagine; ©Jupiter Images; ©Jupiter Images; ©Inmagine; ©Inmagine